# Aerial Imagination in Cuba

T0373688

*Aerial Imagination in Cuba* is a visual, ethnographic, sensorial, and poetic engagement with how Cubans imagine the sky as a medium that allows things to circulate. What do wi-fi antennas, cactuses, pigeons, lottery, and congas have in common? This book offers a series of illustrated ethno-fictional stories to explore various practices and beliefs that have seemingly nothing in common. But if you look at the sky, there is more than meets the eye. By discussing the natural, religious, and human-made visible and invisible aerial infrastructures—or systems of circulation—through short illustrated vignettes, *Aerial Imagination in Cuba* offers a highly creative way to explore the aerial space in Santiago de Cuba today.

**Alexandrine Boudreault-Fournier** is Associate Professor in the Department of Anthropology at the University of Victoria.

**José Manuel Fernández Lavado** is a visual artist, photographer, cameraman, and an audio-visual production instructor based in Cuba.

# Routledge Focus on Anthropology

**The Primate Zoonoses**
Culture Change and Emerging Diseases
*Loretta A. Cormier and Pauline E. Jolly*

**Aerial Imagination in Cuba**
Stories from Above the Rooftops
*Alexandrine Boudreault-Fournier*

For more information about this series, please visit: https://www.routledge.com/anthropology/series/RFA

# Aerial Imagination in Cuba
## Stories from Above the Rooftops

**Alexandrine Boudreault-Fournier**

**Illustrated by**
**José Manuel Fernández Lavado**

**Routledge**
Taylor & Francis Group

LONDON AND NEW YORK

First published 2020 by Routledge

2 Park Square, Milton Park, Abingdon, Oxon, OX14 4RN
605 Third Avenue, New York, NY 10017

*Routledge is an imprint of the Taylor & Francis Group, an informa business*

First issued in paperback 2020

*British Library Cataloguing-in-Publication Data*
A catalogue record for this book is available from the British
Library

*Library of Congress Cataloging-in-Publication Data*
Names: Boudreault-Fournier, Alexandrine, author.
Title: Aerial imagination in Cuba: stories from above the rooftops /
Alexandrine Boudreault-Fournier; illustrated by José Manuel Fernández Lavado.
Description: Abingdon, Oxon; New York, NY: Routledge, [2019] |
Series: Focus on anthropology | Includes bibliographical references and index.
Identifiers: LCCN 2019016390 | ISBN 9781138595958 (hbk: alk. paper) |
ISBN 9780429853319 (pdf) | ISBN 9780429853302 (epub3) |
ISBN 9780429853296 (mobi) | ISBN 9780429456961 (ebk)
Subjects: LCSH: Santiago de Cuba (Cuba)—Social life and customs |
Sky—Social aspects—Cuba—Santiago de Cuba. | Internet—Social
aspects—Cuba—Santiago de Cuba. | Cactus—Social aspects—Cuba—
Santiago de Cuba. | Pigeons—Social aspects—Cuba—Santiago de Cuba. |
Lotteries—Social aspects—Cuba—Santiago de Cuba. | Conga music—
Social aspects—Cuba—Santiago de Cuba.
Classification: LCC F1849.S3 B68 2019 | DDC 972.91/65—dc23
LC record available at https://lccn.loc.gov/2019016390

ISBN: 978-1-138-59595-8 (hbk)
ISBN: 978-0-367-78789-9 (pbk)

Typeset in Times New Roman
by codeMantra

To Noedy, Izak and Lhassa

# Contents

# Illustrations

# Tables

# Acknowledgments

My highest gratitude goes to José Manuel Fernández Lavado, the extremely talented Cuban artist who worked with me on this project. Thank you for moving outside of your comfort zone and for sharing your thoughts and perspectives during our collaboration. In Cuba, I would like to thank the beekeepers, the wi-fi hackers, the pigeon flyers, and all the other people who shared their time and stories with me during my research project in Santiago de Cuba. Our conversations were an immense source of inspiration. You are all present in one way or another in this book. In addition to my family and close friends who appear in the stories recounted in this book—Maria Elena, Edilberto, Marlon, Cuca, Kelli, and Andrea—and other friends who provided an enormous support throughout the years, I wish to thank Inay Rodríguez Agramonte, Vilma Labañino Rodríguez, Ained Martínez, Edislaine Hechavarria Duharte, Roselí Santiesteban Mir, Ariel Reyes Antuan, Raynier Palacio, Maritza Puig, Alayo, and K-merun, as well as my colleague and friend *en la batalla* Yamile Obdulia Haber Guerra. Thank you for always being willing to answer my most obscure questions about Cuba.

Some colleagues have always been present to exchange ideas: Martha Radice, Mélissa Gauthier, Ann Stahl, Karoline Truchon, Kyle Devine, and Francine Saillant. An expert on the Haitian presence in Cuba, Grete Viddal, revised and commented on many versions of this manuscript. Her generous input goes well beyond editorial advising. I was extremely lucky to benefit from her in-depth knowledge of both Cuba and anthropology, as well as her innate sense of storytelling. Thank you so much *querida*. My friend and colleague Nathalie Boucher offered me a space in paradise to write part of this manuscript, which I will always cherish.

I would like to thank Marie-Josée Proulx and Rance Mok for their work on the illustrations. Both are amazing and creative designers and it is always a pleasure working with such professional and talented women. My gratitude to Mark McIntyre for reading earlier versions of the manuscript, Dara Culhane for inviting me at Simon Fraser University to present my early work on this project. The insightful comments of faculty members and students at SFU were appreciated. The Centre for Imaginative Ethnography, an independent research collective exploring creative ethnographic methodologies, always provide inspiration and mental support whilst I cross the "dangerous" line between art and anthropology. To Gabriela McBee, Eleonora Diamanti, and all the students who participated in one of the Cuba Ethnographic Field Schools in 2014, 2016, and 2018: your questions and observations during the field trips were occasions to pause and reflect on many aspects of Cuba that I never thought about or had forgotten throughout the years. We cried and laughed together, we shared memorable moments, and it is a pleasure to follow you as you continue your life journey.

I have great gratitude for the anonymous reviewers at Routledge who took the time to give insightful comments on the manuscript proposal. Thank you to the team at Routledge, Marc Stratton and Katherine Ong who believed in the manuscript project and provided support.

The research conducted for this book was funded by an Insight Development Grant offered by the Social Sciences and Humanities Research Council of Canada and an Internal Research Grant offered by the Faculty of Social Sciences at the University of Victoria.

Both of my parents have influenced me deeply. My father, the linguist Robert Fournier, hired me as a research assistant during the summer of 2000 for his study of the presence of Haitian descendants in Eastern Cuba. This was my first ethnographic experience "in the field" and the beginning of a long and fascinating journey in Cuba. My mother, Diane Boudreault, a visual artist, has inspired me to develop my research and teaching in new and creative directions. This book would not have been possible without my husband Noedy Hechavarria Duharte. Our relationship began on the rooftop of his parents' home, where we constructed a dovecote from scrap wood and chicken wire. Today, Noedy and I have a son, Izak, and a new daughter, Lhassa, and our Cuban-Canadian family thrives with love, friends, and community across borders.

# Introduction

Cubans are deeply devoted to Our Lady of Charity of El Cobre, their patron saint and guardian. The most common image associated with her is that of a glowing Virgin offering protection to three men in a boat whilst hovering above them (Illustration I.1). This visual representation of the story of the first apparition of the Virgin of the Charity and all of its local variations is well known amongst Cubans. Many have an image of the Virgin in their home or a small statue placed on an altar. According to local legend, she first miraculously appeared in the Bay of Nipe, located on the northeast shore of Cuba, in 1612. Two Indigenous brothers and an African slave were looking for salt in a small fishing boat when a storm arose and the ocean quickly turned black and violent. The three men were afraid of capsizing in the turbulent weather. In a state of despair, they began to pray and beg for the protection of the Virgin Mary. Suddenly, the sky cleared and the ocean calmed down. A few meters distant, they noticed a floating object. As they rowed towards it, they realised it was a figurine of the Virgin Mary. She was holding baby Jesus in her left hand and a golden cross in her right hand, and standing on a crescent moon on which was written the following inscription: "I am the Virgin of Charity."

The three men brought the figurine of the Virgin Mary back to land, and a chapel was constructed to host and protect the statue. However, the statue mysteriously disappeared and reappeared on three occasions, which locals and church officials took to mean that the Virgin was not satisfied with her location. Eventually, the figurine was installed in a church located on top of a hill in El Cobre, a copper-mining town (*cobre* means "copper"), which has since become a sacred pilgrimage site for Cubans. Today, the statue is known as Our Lady of Charity of El Cobre or, more affectionately, *Cachita*. The sacred figurine is approximately 61 cm tall and is kept behind glass in the bright yellow sanctuary of El Cobre. The town of El Cobre is only

*Illustration I.1* Common iconography of Our Lady of Charity of El Cobre, the patron saint of Cuba.

12 km from Santiago de Cuba (Cuba's second biggest city, located in the east), but pilgrims travel from all over the country, including the capital, Havana (on the opposite end of the island) to ask the Virgin to intercede in their lives, or to thank her for favours bestowed by laying flowers or wreaths around her statue, lighting candles, or leaving gifts. Cubans hope that the Virgin will protect them from the tempests of life. She is known for her miracle-working powers all over Cuba and is also venerated amongst the Cuban diaspora. There

are many depictions of the Blessed Virgin Mary in Latin American countries—for instance, the Virgin of Guadalupe in Mexico and the Virgin of Mercedes in Peru—but the Virgin of El Cobre is special for Cubans because she is known to be *their* protector and has become the patron saint of Cuba. Our Lady of Charity of El Cobre remains a key symbol of the island's religious complexities, the social imaginary, and Cuban identity today (Portuondo Zúñiga 1995; Díaz 2000; Schmidt 2015).

Because of the significance of this story for Cubans, and the subsequent visual representations that locate the Virgin Mary floating above the three men, the legend of Our Lady of Charity of El Cobre serves as a revealing example of how the sky is everywhere in Cuban religious beliefs and popular culture, including music, cinema, visual arts, and literature. For instance, in "Cuba, qué linda es Cuba" (Cuba, how beautiful is Cuba), a song written in 1959 and recognised as an iconic national favourite, the composer Eduardo Saborit praises Cuba and identifies the sky as one of the island's most striking characteristics. As the song goes, "If you think that our homeland is not that beautiful [...] I invite you to search the world for another sky that is bluer than ours, for a moon as bright as the one that seeps into the sweetness of sugar cane [...]."[1] More recently, the song "Lucas y Lucia," released in 2000 by the well-known and beloved singer-songwriter Carlos Valera, tells the story of two characters who get on a plane to fly north. They fly from a place where people speak Spanish to an English-speaking country. Varela's lyrics use both the Spanish term for sky (*cielo*) and the English word "sky," to signal the crossing of borders, as the protagonists leave their island behind. Lines from the song go (my translation): "They went to the North where everything is available" and "Between the storm and the cloudy sky, they arrived in the land of the forgotten."[2] Many examples can be also found in Cuban cinema. Patricia Ramos' film *El Techo* (On the Roof), which premiered at the December 2016 Havana Film Festival, was shot on the rooftops of Havana. In an interview, Ramos revealed that she is captivated by the universe of the rooftops and used them as a motif to construct a story about young people in Cuba today.[3]

The Cuban sky also inspired me to write this book. I found a muse in my everyday environs, specifically, how Cubans imagine, refer to, and use aerial space. Details that related in one way or another to aerial space came up in conversations, and I began to pay attention to stories about everything from electromagnetics to objects and practices, animals on rooftops, dreams, and sound waves that circulate or resonate above our heads. I came to think of this as constituting a kind of "aerial imagination."

I chose to focus my exploration of the Cuban aerial imagination on five seemingly disparate objects and phenomena: wi-fi antennas, cactuses, pigeons, the lottery, and the conga. The sky became a leitmotif that allowed me to tell five different ethnographically informed stories. As Ingold (2013) suggests, we need an object, a mediator, to *correspond* with the air. The sky can offer a bridge to observe what various eclectic objects and phenomena have in common and also view them through a new lens. Many phenomena in Cuba might turn our gaze to aerial space: children playing with kites on a windy November day, women hanging laundry on a clothesline, tourists enjoying quiet time on a rooftop terrace, musicians playing a concert on an hotel roof bar, young students singing the national anthem as they salute a Cuban flag flapping in the wind... We might also look at the sky for various reasons: to predict the weather, to enjoy (or avoid) the heat of the sun, to orient ourselves in place and time... But hopefully, the five selected objects or phenomena selected and explored in this book demonstrate that the sky is more than just a blue and seemingly empty place above our heads. Instead, it is a territory of intensive communication, transmission, and flow of objects—sometimes invisible—through aerial space.

The five stories presented in the next chapters are based in Santiago de Cuba, a city located on the eastern end of the island. One million people live in the province of Santiago de Cuba, compared to two million in the province of Havana.[4] Cuba is highly centralised, and Havana is the main bureaucratic and administrative hub of the island. The eastern provinces of the island (referred to as *Oriente*) are economically stagnant compared to Havana. Santiago de Cuba is the biggest city in the east; in fact, it is the second biggest city on the island, and it is a cultural and historical focal point for the eastern region. Despite its size, there are few tall buildings in Santiago, and, beyond the centrally located neighborhoods, much of the population lives in apartment complexes of Soviet-style buildings that were constructed around the periphery of the city during the 1970s in an initiative to try to offer housing to every family (see Chapter 2). Santiago de Cuba has a beautiful historical city centre featuring narrow hilly streets that slope down towards a deep bay with a commercial port.

## Illustrated ethno-fiction stories

How Cubans imagine sometimes-invisible phenomenon circulating above their heads might be an abstract notion. And how seemingly disparate objects give shape to cultural systems of circulation and communication might be even more opaque. To shine a light on these ideas, I explore five objects or phenomena in five distinct chapters—wi-fi antennas, cactuses, pigeons, lottery, and conga—through five "illustrated ethno-fiction stories." These vignettes, which merge conversations, observations, and interpretations shared with me whilst I was conducting fieldwork in Santiago de Cuba, are accompanied by a series of drawings. Each of the illustrated stories provides a complex and specific exploration of the sky as a space of motion and imagination, through the lens of a series of characters. My aim is to generate engagement with imaginative ethnography via tales, accounts, and anecdotes I gathered during my decade of fieldwork in Cuba. The five stories are interspersed with historical, social, and economic background information. I also discuss anthropological concerns that are meaningful to the stories, providing a multi-scalar approach to aerial imagination: from the more locally specific, poetic, and personalised, to broader cultural, economic, political, and historical content.

I worked with the Cuban visual artist José Manuel Fernández Lavado to develop the illustrations for the stories. Our aim was to engage *visually* with—often unnoticed—vehicles and pathways that direct our gaze upwards "into the sky and air," forcing us outside of habitual visual orientations. During long sessions of designing, writing, and sketching the illustrated stories, we discussed and exchanged ideas, metaphors, and stories. José Manuel and I have known each other for some time, first working together on a documentary film that I directed in 2010, *Golden Scars*, for which he created the animation, as well as designing the posters and DVD covers. We have maintained contact ever since, and, thanks to the "aerial imagination" book project, we had another opportunity to collaborate. José Manuel Fernández Lavado's input—as a Cuban living in Santiago de Cuba—on the stories we designed was extremely meaningful and significantly impacted the current project. José Manuel added layers of meaning to the stories we fabricated, working together.

In our collaborative work to create each ethno-fiction illustrated story, I would first propose a storyline or script, based on characters, situations, or events I had encountered during my fieldwork. Next, José Manuel added to these stories, contributing his personal anecdotes, comments, and understandings. Then, we worked together on sketches. I often brought photographs to use as a starting point to discuss the perspectives and aesthetics of drawings I envisioned him creating. José Manuel worked on the illustrations, and we met again when he was ready to show the progress of his work.[5] After discussing the drawings and stories, we readjusted, and added or eliminated elements. The illustrated stories for this book emerged as a collaborative work that lasted more than one year. The drawings were finished before I began to write the long versions of the stories.

I am an ethnographic filmmaker, and I approached the creation of these "ethno-fiction illustrated stories" with a cinematic lens. I use the term "ethno-fiction" to echo a genre developed by the French filmmaker and anthropologist Jean Rouch. For him, ethnographic filmmaking involved engagement with imagination and fiction as well as in-depth ethnographic research. Rouch explains that

> For me, as an ethnographer and filmmaker, there is almost no boundary between documentary film and films of fiction. The cinema, the art of the double, is already a transition from the real world to the imaginary world, and ethnography, the science of thought systems of others, is a permanent crossing point from one conceptual universe to another; acrobatic gymnastics where losing one's footing is the least of the risks.
>
> (Rouch in Stoller 1994a:96–97)

A similar blend developed whilst I worked on the illustrated narratives presented in this book. Each illustrated ethno-fiction story produced in collaboration with José Manuel is an independent vignette that delves into an object or a phenomenon that I investigated via observation and informal interviews. Overall, the five illustrated stories address the same question: how do Cubans imagine things circulating in the sky? Each story is a snapshot that explores one phenomenon of the many possibilities swarming in the Cuban sky. These stories allow for poetic, emotional, and personalised discussions of a form of aerial imagination that is meaningful to my Cuban interlocutors.

Similar to filmmaking and video, illustrated ethno-fiction stories engage with issues of narration, representation, and montage. But, in contrast to video, José Manuel's drawings offer more freedom to explore the visible and invisible phenomena circulating in the sky, as well as their poetics and aesthetics. Through the process of writing the script and drawing the stories, the invisible became perceptible and even amplified. For instance, in Chapter 2, the spines of the cactus that protect a household are much longer than what our eyes typically perceive. Like montage techniques in filmmaking, drawings elicit the invisible (Willerslev & Suhr 2013).

Ultimately, I see my participation in this project, together with artist José Manuel, as a mediator. We have transduced (Helmreich 2008) what I heard, observed, and interpreted, with the stories that I wrote, which readers will discover in this book. Research is a creative process (Sullivan 2010), and I fully embrace my role as a creative agent in addition to being a participant observer (Boudreault-Fournier 2012, 2016; Boudreault-Fournier and Wees 2017). This means that I adhere to the expectations associated with the ethnographic enterprise—ethical, methodological, and theoretical—but at the same time, I recognise my role as an interpreter of ethnographic material, inventing illustrated stories that are thus, in part, fiction.

Therefore, *Aerial Imagination in Cuba* offers a critique of "ethnographic authority" and re-envisions how anthropologists construct and impose their ethnographic knowledge (Clifford 1988). These illustrated ethno-fiction stories emerged from constructive negotiations between the participants involved (Clifford 1988), including myself. Anthropologist Karen McCarthy Brown—who also used fiction to expand Haitian family stories shared with her when writing the ethnography *Mama Lola: A Vodou Priestess in Brooklyn*—noted that white Euro-American social scientific tradition has an obsession with accuracy and "truth" (McCarthy Brown 2010:19). Anthropologists have not escaped from the modernist quest for objectivism and realism. Yet, similar to a West African griot who tells a story about an event or a person with respect and depth (Stoller 1994b), my fabrications bridge with what I learned during my ethnographic experiences in order to create the stories I present in these chapters.

I could not have written the following stories without long-term immersion and in-depth field investigations in Cuba. Similarly, the anthropologist Paul Stoller, in a note at the end of his first novel, titled *Jaguar: A Story of Africans in America* (1999), writes that without his 33 years of ethnographic field research in Niger, the novel would never have seen the light of day. In writing *Jaguar*, Stoller (1999:12) explains that he wished to delve into the topics of love, regret, and social obligation, which lend themselves well to fiction. In the preface of his second novel, *Gallery Bundu* (2005), Stoller announces that the book is a work of fiction and explains that the characters in the novel are composites of various people he met during his research in the field. This is similar to the approach I adopted for *Aerial Imagination in Cuba*.

In the footsteps of Jean Rouch and other filmmaker-anthropologists such as Johannes Sjöberg (2008), I also had previous experience with ethno-fiction cinema. I co-directed, with two Brazilian colleagues, the film *Fabrik Funk* (2015).[6] Similar to Stoller, we clearly announced the fictional nature of the characters and the plot of the film in the credits, whilst also mentioning that many elements came from our ethnographic observations and interpretations. Producing an ethno-fiction film allowed us to explore, through drama, topics that were directly connected to our ethnographic research—popular youth culture on the outskirts of São Paulo and emerging musical practices—at the same time as we remained open to spontaneous encounters and discoveries emerging from the involvement of young actor-participants who contributed to the project (Boudreault-Fournier, Hikiji Gitirana and Caiuby Novaes 2016a, 2016b).

Each vignette from *Aerial Imagination in Cuba* corresponds to a condensed version of characters and accounts that I heard and observed whilst I conducted ethnographic fieldwork in Santiago de Cuba. None of the stories reflect only one character. My protagonists are compilations of stories and observations gathered throughout years, and mirror my own interpretations and creative agency. Thus, the characters represented in these illustrated stories are in part fictional. Some names were changed, and visual appearances were transformed. Yet, I could not help but to create characters based on people who are part of my personal life in Cuba. My desire was to locate the stories as belonging to *my* experiences and history in Cuba, the conversations I had with friends, and the relations I constructed since I first began fieldwork in Cuba in 2000. All these encounters contribute to who I am today: a white Canadian woman, a passionate anthropologist, a filmmaker, and a mother married to a Cuban man whose family lives in Santiago de Cuba.

## Cuba in a time of transition

This book locates the Cuban aerial imagination in a time of rapid transformation. A few significant elements highlighting Cuban context and history need to be addressed in order to fully grasp what these changes imply for Cubans today. Most notably, Fidel Castro and his followers declared the beginning of the Cuban Revolution 60 years ago, on January 1, 1959. The new regime ended years of dictatorship under U.S.-backed dictator Fulgencio Batista and U.S. intervention in Cuban economic and political affairs. The U.S. implemented a full economic embargo against Cuba in 1962 that included almost all imports. As a result of the embargo, Cuba eventually developed economic relationships with the Soviet Union as well as countries that supported socialist initiatives (for instance, Mozambique, Angola, China, and

Venezuela). Whilst the embargo still continues today, the movement of people and goods between the U.S. and Cuba are being re-imagined. The Cuban political system is characterised by a state-centred socialist economic system and a one-party-rule dictatorship, and the state is supported by a strong nationalist and revolutionary discourse expressed through various state bodies. During the collapse of the Soviet Union at the beginning of the 1990s, Cuba witnessed its most severe economic crisis since the beginning of the Cuban Revolution. The crisis associated with the loss of Soviet subsidies is commonly referred to as the "Special Period." In order to rebuild its economy, the Cuban government developed its tourist industry and opened its borders to private investment (amongst other policies).[7] The tourist industry became a motor of the Cuban economy. But this policy also fuelled the growth of social problems. Poverty, prostitution, and hustling for tourist dollars inaugurated a deepening of the economic disparities between white Cubans and Afro-Cubans. Retrospectively, many older Cubans remember the revolutionary system as having had its good and bad times. For instance, the 1970s, with nascent Soviet economic subsidies, are remembered as a time of hope. The 1980s are often remembered as a kind of "golden era" during which even working-class Cubans could afford modest indulgences, such as ice cream or a Sunday meal at a restaurant. But the collapse of the Soviet Union as Cuba's main trading partner inaugurated a difficult economic period in the early 1990s.

Periods of limited access to goods and lack of diversity on the official market, reflect socialist systems' widespread perception as "economies of shortage" (Verdery 1996:21). In this context, extensive underground quasi-legal and illegal economies sprang up in Cuba in response to shortages of goods on the official market. Verdery (1996:27) argues that both official and secondary economies are interconnected, implying that they are mutually dependent. Extensive social networks based on barter, bribes, exchanges, and obligations helped Cubans resolve everyday problems. It is no exaggeration to say that in such contexts, social relationships and networks are often more useful than money when it comes to acquiring food or consumer goods. As a consequence, socialist systems generate different approaches to the notion of value compared to capitalist models (Humphrey & Hugh-Jones 1992:5).

The average monthly salary for employees of the Cuban government— such as civil servants, teachers and university professors, health sector professionals, garbage collectors, and public transportation workers—ranges approximately from USD 15 to 30 per month. This salary is hardly enough to survive in contemporary Cuba. The price of consumer goods, including clothing, shoes, and hygiene products (shampoo, soap, toothpaste, etc.), is similar to the cost of such products sold in North America and Europe. Also, vegetables, meat, and fish are expensive and not affordable for many Cubans. At the beginning of the Revolution, a food-rationing programme was initiated. Cuban families all received a share of basic staples at a very low cost, for example sugar, meat, cigarettes, coffee, flour, salt, and cooking oil. However, since the post-Soviet "Special Period," the products offered on the ration card are not sufficient to cover minimal food needs. So Cubans invent (*inventar*) alternative ways to generate money in what could be called a black or grey (illegal or semi-legal) economy. They might offer services, import clothing, sell home-made yogurt, pastries, popsicles, or *churros* in the streets or from their homes, or re-sell pilfered state commodities, etc. In 2010, after announcing layoffs of more than 500,000 government employees, the Cuban Ministry of Labor and Social Security cautiously allowed some sectors of the economy to privatise (Resolution 32/2010). For the first time since the beginning of the Revolution, it became legal to own a small business and hire employees. The legalisation of small enterprises extended to 178 occupations, including barber, carpenter, artisan, animal caretaker, owner of a Bed and Breakfast (*casa particular*), a small restaurant (*paladar*), or snack bar (*cafeteria*). These small-scale private businesses allow many Cubans to earn a better living than working for the public sector. And the tourist industry offers amongst the best working conditions, which explains why there is a "brain drain" of professionals (dentists, teachers, doctors, etc.) who prefer working in hotels or as tour guides rather than in their respective fields. Cubans deal with two national currencies that generally correspond to two types of stores and services: the peso Cubano (CUP) in which government salaries are paid, and the convertible Cuban peso (CUC) a kind of faux hard-currency used in the tourist industry and to purchase luxury or imported goods.

Fidel Castro finally resigned as Head of State on February 18, 2008, citing health issues. His successor was his brother Raúl Castro, who initially sparked hopes of gradual improvement amongst Cubans eager for better living conditions and an opening to international relationships in both areas of trade and communication. As a direct response to a shared desire for more economic and social freedom, Raúl Castro indeed lifted what he called "excessive prohibitions," particularly on electronics and communication and small businesses. As a consequence, for the first time in the country's history, at the end of

March 2008, Cubans were legally permitted to purchase cell phones, computers, DVD players, and other devices such as toasters and microwaves. Also lifted were legal restrictions prohibiting Cubans from lodging in tourist hotels and renting cars. In 2011, reforms allowed Cubans to buy property. In 2013, they were allowed to travel abroad without requiring exit permits from the Cuban authorities.

Announcements of greater public access to internet gave clear indications that Cubans would increasingly have access to digital data. A fibre-optic cable arrived in Cuba from Venezuela in 2011, and promised a high-speed connection for the population at large. But because national internet infrastructure was still dependent on substandard equipment and expensive satellites, the Venezuelan cable has not yet acceded to increasing Cuban demand. As a result, it is still difficult and costly to access the internet in Cuba, and the country continues to have considerably lower internet penetration rates than most other countries globally, although this is changing (see Chapter 1). On December 17, 2014, then U.S. President Barack Obama and the Cuban head of state Raúl Castro announced that they would progressively normalise political, economic, and diplomatic relationships between the two countries, providing hope for change to all Cuban citizens. Unfortunately, this initiative did not deliver the hoped-for results, mainly because of the status quo orientation adopted by the subsequent U.S. President Donald Trump. Raúl Castro resigned on April 2018. For the first time since 1959, the newly appointed President of Cuba—Miguel Díaz-Canel—was not a member of the Castro family. At the end of 2018, the Cuban National Assembly approved a revised version of the Cuban constitution, which although it retained the one-party socialist system as the guiding force of the country, also recognised the importance of foreign investment. All evidence shows that Cuba is in the midst of a major sociopolitical transition.

## Overview of the book

Each chapter develops one main story based on one object or phenomenon representing a snapshot of how Cubans imagine life unfolding in the sky. Embedded in the stories, relevant historical, social, and economic background is provided to situate the reader within contemporary Cuba.

Isaac, a modern-day Cuban hacker who managed to pirate official wi-fi connections and redistribute them at a cheaper price to potential navigators, is the first character of the book. His ingenuity in playing with aerial media wi-fi connections is impressive and shows the creativity of Cubans when coping with scarcity. Issac's story encourages readers to "rotate" their sights towards the sky and, more specifically, to pay attention to the alternative networks developed by Cubans to access the internet and to respond to the digital scarcity, as wi-fi antennas placed in parks and other public spaces in Santiago de Cuba act as magnets around which people concentrate to access the best connections.

In the next chapter, cactuses placed on rooftops are used to push away "bad waves," or what Cubans call the *mala vista* (translated as "evil eye"). In this story, protagonist Maria Elena struggles to construct a house for herself and her family in spite of material shortages and economic constraints. After a series of bad luck events, she realises that she needs a cactus to protect her household against the evil eye that prevents her from advancing her construction project. This chapter dives into the religious forces attached to the cactus and depicts this little plant as an inhibitor of circulation (in comparison to wi-fi antennas, which disperse circulation).

In the third chapter, I tell the story of 12-year-old Marlon, a boy who raises pigeons on the rooftop of his house. Some pigeon-keepers dedicate themselves to racing, whilst others own pigeons just for the passion of raising the birds. Marlon is a young and inexperienced pigeon owner, but he has high expectations for his favourite bird, and wants to train it to become a great racer. Science still knows little about how pigeons are able to fly back home over long distances. Some researchers suggest that homing pigeons have an internal map or innate perception of where they are located and where they are going. How will Marlon's pigeon fly back home from far away?

Chapter 4 further develops the ideas of luck and hope—already touched upon in Chapter 2—to discuss the lottery in Cuba. Called *la bolita* (small ball) in Cuba, the lottery is illegal but that does not stop Edilberto from playing once in a while, mainly when he feels a *cábala* (a strong revelation, dream, or event) that grabs his attention enough to warrant a bet. The winning *bolita* numbers are announced through radio waves from Miami and transmitted all over Cuba. Both the winning numbers and the *cábala* travel through the air to make the *bolita*, or lottery, a very successful, if illegal, game.

Congas are spontaneous parades of people walking, dancing, and singing in the streets, led by an ensemble of percussionists. The most famous conga in Santiago de Cuba is called the Conga Los Hoyos. The congas are unpredictable. They can emerge at any time of day or evening, and they can be provoked by events, such as the Santiago de Cuba baseball team winning a game. Congas, which are also common during the Carnival in July, are very loud, and it is the contagious rhythms of the drums travelling to Kelly's ears that convince her to join the parade despite her mother's admonishments.

In looking at the sky, we perceive a space or medium through which things circulate. The narrative arc of the book shows how there is more to the sky than meets the eye. If we look carefully, we will discover a range of things circulating, including electromagnetic waves, animals, beliefs, and sounds.

## Notes

1 The original lyrics in Spanish: "Oye, tú que dices que tu patria no es tan linda [...] Yo te invito a que busques por el mundo, Otro cielo más azul como tu cielo. Una luna tan brillante como aquella, Que se filtra en la dulzura de la caña."
2 The original lyrics in Spanish: "Lucas y Lucía eran dos enanos / se fueron un día en un aeroplano. Donde acaba el cielo, comienza el sky se fueron al Norte, "donde todo lo hay". / "Y buscaban y buscaban / nada más, un sitio donde / al menos poder respirar. [...] / Y también del Norte se escaparon / y con su aeroplano se largaron. / Entre la tormenta y el cielo nublado / llegaron a tierras de los olvidados."
3 Mayté Madruga Hernández, n.d. "El techo, una pelicula aterizada." Available on the website of Cubacine: El Portal del ICAIC, www.cubacine. cult.cu/articulo/2016/12/15/techo-una-pelicula-aterrizada. The interview was taken from the Havana Festival website.
4 Oficina Nacional de Estadística e información, República de Cuba, censo 2012. www.one.cu/resumenadelantadocenso2012.htm. According to this census, approximately 500,000 people live in the city of Santiago de Cuba.
5 To watch José Manuel in progress: https://vimeo.com/164956977.
6 The two co-directors are Rose Hikiji Satiko Gitirana and Sylvia Caiuby Novaes. The English version of the film *Fabrik Funk* is available at this address: https://vimeo.com/121777735.
7 For a thorough review of key challenges and issues related to the "Special Period," see the introduction by Ariana Hernandez-Reguant (2009) in her edited volume on the same topic.

## References

Boudreault-Fournier, Alexandrine. 2012. "Écho d'une rencontre virtuelle: Vers une ethnographie de la production audio-visuelle." *Anthropologica* 54(1):1–12.
Boudreault-Fournier, Alexandrine. 2016. "Microtopia in Counterpoint: Relational Aesthetics and the Echo Project." *Cadernos de Arte e Antropologia* 5(1):135–154.

Boudreault-Fournier, Alexandrine and Nick Wees. 2017. "Creative Engagement with Interstitial Urban Spaces: The Case of the Vancouver's Back Alleys." In *Urban Encounters: Art and the Public*, edited by Martha Radice and Alexandrine Boudreault-Fournier. Montreal: McGill University Press, pp. 192–211.

Boudreault-Fournier, Alexandrine, Rose Hikiji and Sylvia Caiuby Novaes. 2016a. "Fabriquer le funk à Cidade Tiradentes, São Paulo: la performance d'une ethnofiction." *Cultures-Kairós* no. 7. http://revues.mshparisnord.org/cultureskairos/index.php?id=1439.

Boudreault-Fournier, Alexandrine, Rose Hikiji and Sylvia Caiuby Novaes. 2016b. "Etnoficção. Uma ponte entre fronteiras." In *A Experiência da imagem na etnografia*, edited by Andrea Barbosa, Edgar Teodoro Da Cunha, Rose Satiko Gitirana and Sylvia Caiuby Novaes. São Paulo: Editora Terceiro Nome LTDA, pp. 37–58.

Clifford, James. 1988. *The Predicament of Culture: Twentieth-Century Ethnography, Literature, and Art*. Cambridge, MA: Harvard University Press.

Díaz, María Elena. 2000. *The Virgin, The King, and The Royal Slaves of El Cobre: Negotiating Freedom in Colonial Cuba, 1670–1780*. Stanford: Stanford University Press.

Helmreich, Stefan. 2008. "An Anthropologist Underwater: Immersive Soundscapes, Submarine Cyborgs, and Transductive Ethnography." *American Ethnologist* 34(4):621–641.

Hernandez-Reguant, Ariana. 2009. "Writing the Special Period: An Introduction." In *Cuba in the Special Period: Culture and Ideology in the 1990s*, edited by Ariana Hernandez-Reguant. New York: Palgrave Macmillian, pp. 1–18.

Humphrey, Caroline and Stephen Hugh-Jones. 1992. "Introduction: Barter, Exchange, and Value." In *Barter, Exchange and Value: An Anthropological Approach*, edited by Caroline Humphrey and Stephen Hugh-Jones. Cambridge: Cambridge University Press, pp. 1–21.

Ingold, Tim. 2013. *Making: Anthropology, Archaeology, Art and Architecture*. New York: Routledge.

McCarthy Brown, Karen. 2010. *Mama Lola: A Vodou Priestess in Brooklyn*. Berkeley: University of California Press.

Portuondo Zúñiga, Olga. 1995. *La Virgen de la Caridad: símbolo de cubanía*. Santiago de Cuba: Editorial Oriente.

Schmidt, Jalane D. 2015. *Cachita's Streets: The Virgin of Charity, Race, and Revolution in Cuba*. Durham: Duke University Press.

Sjöberg, Johannes. 2008. "Ethnofiction: Drama as a Creative Research Practice in Ethnographic Film." *Journal of Media Practice* 9(3):229–242.

Stoller, Paul. 1994a. "Artaud, Rouch and the Cinema of Cruelty." In *Visualizing Theory: Selected Essays from V.A.R. 1990–1994*, edited by Lucien Taylor. New York: Routledge, pp. 84–98.

Stoller, Paul. 1994b. "Ethnographies as Texts / Ethnographers as Griots." *American Ethnologist* 21(2):353–366.

Stoller, Paul. 1999. *Jaguar: A Story of Africans in America.* Chicago: The University of Chicago Press.

Stoller, Paul. 2005. *Gallery Bundu.* Chicago: The University of Chicago Press.

Sullivan, Graeme. 2010. *Art Practice as Research: Inquiry in Visual Arts.* London: Sage.

Verdery, Katherine. 1996. *What was Socialism, and what Comes Next?* Princeton: Princeton University Press.

Willerslev, Rane and Christian Suhr. 2013. "Introduction: Montage as an Amplifier of Invisibility." In *Transcultural Montage,* edited by Christian Suhr and Rane Willerslev. New York: Berghahn Books, pp. 1–15.

# 1 Wi-Fi

A recent event forced me to shift my ethnographic gaze from the more common horizontal way of seeing to a more vertical form of observation. On the 1st of July 2015, wi-fi antennas were installed in more than 300 public spaces all over Cuba, mainly in parks and plazas. This allowed Cubans to have access to legal wi-fi internet connections *for the first time*. In Santiago de Cuba, wi-fi antennas were installed in four main areas of the city: three in parks and one in a popular pedestrian boulevard. As part of my research project on media infrastructure in Cuba, I first began to investigate how wi-fi connections alter the ways in which Cubans hang out in parks and public spaces, and second, how they imagine the wi-fi signals travelling from the antennas to their smartphone and laptop devices. Because of the wi-fi antennas (and the phenomena associated with them), my gaze increasingly turned towards the sky. Cubans began to talk to me about wi-fi antennas and how the locations of the antennas in the park influence where they sit and stand to access the best signals. Three wi-fi antennas were fixed on the wall at the bottom of the cathedral in Céspedes Park, the central and busiest park of the city. Many Cubans began to stand in front of the cathedral, not because of a divine call, but because of their desire to catch the best wi-fi signals (Illustration 1.1).

Before embarking on the "aerial imagination" project, which directed my gaze upwards, I did not even know what a wi-fi antenna looked like. I imagined it probably had a similar shape to an analogue TV antenna. I quickly found out that it is nothing like a TV antenna; instead, it looks like a white or grey flat chocolate box. In North America and Europe, wi-fi antennas are everywhere. We rarely notice them, but Cubans do, and they search for them in public spaces all the time.

It was my new gaze, rotated skyward, provoked by the wi-fi antennas, that inspired the idea for this book. This shift of angle in how I looked at the world around me and whether I oriented straight ahead, or up,

*Illustration 1.1* Wi-fi antenna in Céspedes Park at night-time.

or down, deeply altered how I began to conceive the ways in which often invisible media, including wi-fi signals, circulate. Thanks to my upward gaze, urban spaces that I never significantly noticed before came to my attention, such as spaces located above the street, on top of buildings, and in the sky. We rarely stop to consider the elevated spaces that make up urban centres, such as rooftops, balconies, and terraces—despite significant social activities associated with them.

When I met with José Manuel, the Cuban artist who drew the illustrations for this book, to discuss the "aerial imagination" project for the first time, the idea of developing a story about wi-fi antennas came naturally. The character who will lead us into the mysterious world of Cuban internet and the business of illicit wi-fi connections is named Isaac.

Isaac started a degree in electrical engineering at the University of Oriente in Santiago de Cuba, but he dropped his courses before the end of his first year. He left university, not because he was not talented, but because he was bored by the material covered in class and also because he found his studies disconnected from his life. Isaac is a natural entrepreneur who is always looking for ways to make money. He applies his knowledge of electronics and computer sciences in impressive and creative ways. For instance, he has a neighbourhood word-of-mouth business fixing computers invaded by viruses or in need of upgrades. Isaac is a good example of how Cubans in general cope resourcefully with a precarious economic situation, compounded by the U.S. embargo. Cubans use words like "inventing" (*inventar*) or "resolving" (*resolver*), when fixing problems or coming up with alternative products, patterns, or systems for getting things done. In fact, fundamentally speaking, the

Cuban Revolution itself, with its values and its models, defiantly challenges the predominant capitalist model. In response to the U.S. and international embargo of the socialist island, the Cuban government promotes and funds local development of pharmaceutical generics and encourages the use of natural medicine, including locally produced herbal remedies and acupuncture, because purchasing medicines from pharmaceutical corporations in other countries is prohibitively expensive. In addition, computer laboratories provide the Cuban population with Linux and other free software. This is in part to achieve technological independence. For example, Nova, an operating system funded by the Cuban state and developed by the University of Information Sciences in Havana, was launched in 2009. These are only a few examples of alternative products, networks, and systems promoted by the Cuban government. Isaac echoes this general tendency of responding to scarcity in ingenuous ways. One day, Isaac told me that "inventing" is a way of life in Cuba, as citizens have no choice but to cope with scarcity—food, hygiene products, transportation, communication, money, etc.—in creative ways as a matter of survival.[1]

Isaac's mother is a doctor. She spent two years in Brazil on a "medical mission," a programme whereby the Cuban government sends medical personnel to other countries. Thanks to this, she was able to purchase and import from Brazil a desktop computer for the family. Isaac quickly monopolised the computer to play video games (a pirated version of *Call of Duty* being his favourite, Illustration 1.2). Despite owning a computer, it was impossible for Isaac to access the internet, a service that is still not available in his neighbourhood. Yet, his desire to play online with his friends who also owned computers (not common in Santiago) drove him to develop an alternative system to connect various PCs located in different houses. In a country where access to the internet is extremely limited, connectivity is something Cubans do not take for granted.

Only a minority of the Cuban population has regular internet access. Also, access rates are low outside the capital, Havana, particularly in rural areas and in the eastern provinces of the island. Until recently, internet has been carefully controlled, providing only certain people (for instance, doctors, students, and professionals) the right to have an email account within a national system (intranet), and, less frequently, an international account. Very few have internet at home, and their connections, until very recently, relied exclusively on a dial-up system. Suppliers of illegal internet connections risked long-term jail sentences if caught. Until the beginning of the 2010s, only foreigners could use the internet in hotels and ETECSA[2] offices. But in May 2013, the Cuban government inaugurated 118 internet stations, placing them inside state-owned ETECSA offices located

*Illustration 1.2* Isaac plays video games "online."

all over the island (ETECSA is the only internet provider in Cuba). For the equivalent of USD 4.50 per hour, the state provided would-be web surfers with ID cards, registered by their local ETECSA office, and, finally, Cubans could legally browse the internet on one of the ETECSA's PCs. However, given that typical Cuban state salaries range between USD 15 and 30 per month, a price of USD 4.50 per hour was accessible only to Cubans with non-state sources of income (such as families receiving remittances from abroad, those working in the tourist industry earning tips in hard-currency, or folks with "grey market" or "black market" businesses offering everything from tours to Bed and Breakfasts to private restaurants to salsa lessons to non-licenced renovation to imported goods) operating in informal economies. But as mentioned before, it was not until 2015 that legal wi-fi connections in public spaces became available to the Cuban population. As time passed, more antennas were installed in varied public spaces and internet service became cheaper. During the summer of 2018, Cubans could purchase a wi-fi connection card for USD 1.50, which gave them a one-hour connection. There are also illicit vendors who offer one-hour wi-fi connection for a discount: only USD 1.00. In Cuba, a 50-cent difference in price is meaningful. We will learn more about these illicit wi-fi venders in this story.

The prices for internet services have dropped each year since the Cuban government first began to offer legal connectivity to the general population. For instance, in 2017, it was announced that ETECSA would begin to offer home internet connectivity following a successful pilot project called Nauta Hogar, which was first launched in the historic district of Havana and later expanded across the island. Nauta Hogar offers 30 hours of wi-fi internet connection at different speeds (kbps) for prices ranging from USD 15 to 70 per month. The service is available only to clients who already own a home landline (see Chapter 5). In December 2018, ETECSA began to sell the 3G service—internet on cell phones—which can be purchased starting at USD 7 for up to 300 MB of download capacity. But, again, given the official average salary for even a skilled professional in the public sector, much less a lower-paid manual worker, internet access remains out of reach for a large segment of the population.

Whilst the internet has become increasingly available in Cuba, it has been through a pay system that accentuates disparities between those who can afford the internet and those who cannot. Freedom House, an American watchdog organisation dedicated to freedom and democracy around the globe, estimates that 5%–26% of the Cuban population had access to the internet in 2014.[3] According to the same organisation, Cuban internet penetration rates increased to 38.8% in 2018.[4] Despite this impressive increase, internet connections remain unreliable, patchy, slow, and expensive. The media scholar Cristina Venegas argues that three principal motives can explain why the internet was not (and still is not) accessible to the majority of the Cuban population—namely, political, financial, and infrastructural (Venegas 2010, 58; also see Recio Silva 2014). Venegas argues that "Whether or not the Internet ... may be a threat to Cuba's own democratic aspirations, it is surely so perceived by the government" (2010:185). Still, the recent increases in connectivity options mean that, overall, Cubans have more opportunities to access email, keeping in touch with family or friends abroad via apps like IMO or Facebook Messenger, and digital data including music, films, and digitally available newspapers and websites.

As Cubans get in touch with their families and friends living abroad through the internet, parks with wi-fi connections are transformed into hotspots where people can communicate with those outside the island. Most Cubans go online knowing that they have a limited time to navigate. This creates a sense of hurry and stress as the seconds (and money) fly away. Such a phenomenology of the internet is something few in the global north can identify with—at least today.

Alternative networks have emerged to counter the inefficiency and unreliability of the official state-run media infrastructures in Cuba. One of them is the *paquete*, a weekly digital media package distributed through memory sticks and other portable devices, that allows Cubans to access music files and videos, films, telenovelas, talk-shows, and other audio-visual products such as documentaries. The *paquete* also includes lists of ads for new and used items (from computers to memory sticks to dogs) for sale by individuals, as well as services being offered, similar to the site Craigslist. The *paquete* providers use various illicit strategies, including downloading data from internet connections in or near hotels via cable and copying data from illicit antennas to a VCR or computer. Some providers also receive weekly *paquete* content from the U.S. through antennas. The weekly *paquete* is approximately 800–900 GB, and the price is established according to the weight of digital data transferred onto the client's device. If bought in its entirety, the *paquete* currently costs USD 1.00.

Isaac buys the *paquete* from his neighbour every Tuesday morning when it becomes available in Santiago de Cuba. He does not really know how his provider accesses the weekly *paquete* (and nobody seems to know!), but he thinks that the hard drive with all of the digital content travels from Havana to Santiago by interprovincial bus, with some drivers transporting the *paquete* on their routes in order to augment their incomes via the black market. Every Tuesday morning, new digital files spread amongst *paquete* venders and the content becomes available to the general Cuban population. Isaac empties his memory stick every week to allow the transfer of new digital material. He particularly likes to watch Hollywood films. Those spread like gunfire all over the island, even whilst they are still in cinema theatres outside Cuba.[5] Isaac acquires the video games he plays via the *paquete*, it is how gamers keep track of the new gaming trends, such as Fortnite. There are no video game stores in Cuba and no way for Cubans to purchase international games legally on the island—video games are pirated and shared through the *paquete*, memory sticks, and hard drives.

In order to play "online," but without having access to the internet, Isaac decided to connect his gaming friends using ethernet cables (Illustration 1.3). Before the ubiquity of wi-fi antennas in North America and Europe, the basic thick blue ethernet cable used to be the fastest way to connect to the internet and download images. Now, that same cable serves as the means not only to connect Isaac with his friends but also to build what is called in Cuba the *intranet callejera* (the intranet of the street), or Street Net (SNET).[6] This network offers an impressive alternative infrastructure connecting many people (sometimes up to 200 houses per network) and allowing Cubans to share digital data, news, and information, to chat on VIPBook (a Cuban version of Facebook) and to play games—including one of Cuba's favourite pastimes, dominoes. Thus, the SNET is a Cuban alternative version of the internet, deconstructing the often taken-for-granted idea that

*Illustration 1.3* Isaac connects with his gaming friends using ethernet cables.

there exists only "one" internet. Houses are connected through ethernet cables that converge at the home of a "server," which corresponds to someone who owns a "switch" (or a router) and serves as centralising station for the connections. It is thanks to this network that Isaac and his friends play their favourite games "online." But again, this system does not connect Cubans to the World Wide Web. Instead, it creates an alternative internet, actually an intranet, or system of digital file sharing, amongst the connected users only.

But the SNET story does not end there. Sometimes, the home of a server is connected to an access point (generally called an AP or a WAP, a wireless access point), which is a hidden wi-fi antenna placed on a rooftop (Illustration 1.4). This wi-fi antenna is connected to other wi-fi antennas—which, in turn, connect another set of users linked through ethernet cables, and so on. The city of Santiago is enveloped by such invisible webs of homemade ethernet/wi-fi networks. This is a reminder that infrastructures are relational and "ecological," that they both shape and are shaped by the conventions of a community of practice (Leigh-Star 1999). With a little bit of attention and by directing our gaze towards the sky, we can observe the blue cables hanging over roofs and attached to walls all over Santiago. Cubans may also dig

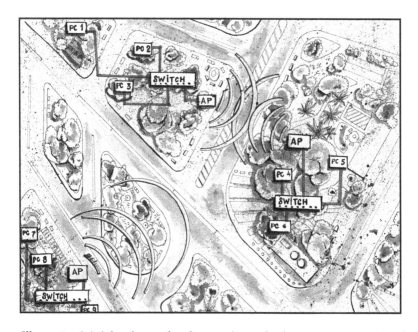

*Illustration 1.4* A local map showing an alternative internet system made of ethernet cables and illicit wi-fi antennas.

across the middle of a street to pass an ethernet cable under the pavement to connect two neighbours facing each other. These practices are somewhat tolerated by state authorities, although they are most often performed discretely at night-time to avoid any problem. The SNET falls within a legal grey area; the authorities do not seem to know how to address the issue, at least not yet. Illicit wi-fi antennas are often hidden behind houses and are difficult to observe from the street. Cubans who are connected through ethernet cables tend to be quiet about their apparatus and activities. But they believe that it is only a matter of time before these practices will be legally prohibited and punished. An indicator of this is that wi-fi antennas are imported illegally onto the island, and the ethernet cables used by the SNET users are typically stolen from state-owned warehouses and sold on the black market.

Isaac successfully connected 5 of his close friends and 42 neighbours, thanks to ethernet cables. He charges them ten Cuban pesos (USD 50 cents) per month for the SNET service. In addition to providing the connection, he also shares digital files he acquires through the *paquete* with his network users. To join his network, one has to provide and install the ethernet cable up to Isaac's house, and he takes care of the rest. Isaac also offers technical help and basic navigation workshops.

In Cuba, technologically savvy self-taught computer technicians like Isaac, who could be called "hackers," depend on the willingness of their peers to share their knowledge. Cubans excel at inventing ways to pirate and share digital material including music, films, and telenovelas. In referring to copied digital media and video games distributed through memory sticks, Isaac told me that computer hackers in Cuba "are the *real* pirates of the Caribbean, authorized by the pirate in chief [Fidel Castro]. Johnny Depp can go back home; *he* is the copy; *we* are the original ones!".

Without easy access to information online or YouTube videos on "how to hack a wi-fi connection," the direct physical sharing of information amongst "hackers" becomes the main way to develop robust alternatives and to deal with digital scarcity. It is thanks to this collegiality that Isaac placed all the pieces of the puzzle together and acquired the tools on the black market to pirate the ETECSA wi-fi antennas located below the cathedral of Céspedes Park. Each antenna has a capacity to serve 50 simultaneous users connecting through their phone or laptop. This means that no more than 50 users can connect to the internet simultaneously when using the official ETECSA card wi-fi service. When the park is very busy, mainly at night-time, it is not rare to spend hours just trying to connect to the wi-fi service, because it is overloaded by users and as a consequence, slow and unreliable.

Isaac acquired a router on the black market, and his friend Juan contributed to his entrepreneurial initiative by lending him his laptop. Without losing ourselves in the technical details involved in this hacking practice, we will focus on how the steps taken by Isaac to sell illicit wi-fi connections demonstrate the ingenuity of Cubans when coping with digital scarcity. Isaac purchased various pay-as-you-go cards from ETECSA to connect Juan's laptop to the official state internet server. Thanks to his router and a pirated programme he installed on his computer called Connectify Hotspot, he retransmitted the ETECSA signals to allow other users to connect to the internet via his own system of distribution (Illustration 1.5). In other words, he became an illicit provider of internet by pirating and reselling the official wi-fi signals of ETECSA .

*Illustration 1.5* Isaac at his wi-fi reselling station in Céspedes Park.

For USD 1 (USD 50 cents cheaper than the official ETECSA card), Isaac offers a comparable service to the one provided by ETECSA.[7] The client pays Isaac directly for the service at the beginning of the session. The income Isaac makes is substantial. His business costs include the legal ETECSA access cards he purchases, and the 10% of his daily revenues he pays for the use of his friend Juan's laptop.

Every night, Isaac makes his way to the park with his friend's laptop and his router (Illustration 1.6). Because the wi-fi connection he offers does not necessitate an access card, many find that his service is more convenient. Long lines to purchase an internet card at the ETECSA offices during normal working hours are common and extremely time-consuming. Instead, with Isaac, clients can avoid lines and interact directly with him. He always stands close to the laptop and the

*Illustration 1.6* Clients of Isaac surfing the World Wide Web.

router, and people know who he is. Isaac does not give the password to access his router; instead, he enters the password himself in the cellular or laptop of his client and keeps track of who is connected and makes sure that no one spends more time online than what they have paid for. There is no law that officially prohibits this activity, at least not yet. The wi-fi venders do not hide their equipment, but there is definitely a sense that what they do is not 100% legitimate. There are periods during which venders are persecuted by the police and even arrested for stealing and commercialising wi-fi connections, and other periods during which their activities are tolerated. But according to Isaac, it is just a matter of time before new laws officially prohibit the reselling of wi-fi connections (recently, some venders I know have been formally accused despite the absence of official laws).

But for now, Isaac's hacking strategy is working. In the same manner as Robin Hood, Isaac redistributes the internet connection provided by the Cuban government's communication "kingdom" to the poor who are hungry to surf the net. Yet, Isaac is not the only skilled pirate in Santiago de Cuba. Other hackers, who might not share the same collegiality mentioned earlier, also fight to secure a spot in the illicit wi-fi connection business.

Day after day, Isaac unpacks his equipment and stands in the same corner of Céspedes Park. His consistent location helps his clients to easily find him. His seniority in this business gives him the privilege of picking the best location, which is just below the three ETECSA antennas fixed on the wall of the cathedral. Isaac knows that he cannot miss one day of work, as he risks that other hackers will steal his spot and his clients. Location is key to this business because clients are in search of the best connections. A kind of code of silence amongst the wi-fi connection hackers dictates these rules. However, Isaac was about to learn that not all hackers follow the same principles.

One of the busiest evenings of the year is Mother's Day, and Isaac was focused on connecting his clients and keeping track of those who were already connected. Without him noticing it, two hackers unpacked their equipment and began to offer wi-fi connections inside of Isaac's territory (Illustration 1.7). These two men, whom Isaac knew from his neighbourhood, were actually stealing aerial space from Isaac and the wi-fi signals travelling through it. Isaac's clients began to complain that the connection was slow and unreliable. The connection was obviously overloaded. The two extra buffoons were causing the situation. It was the most lucrative evening of the year, and Isaac was determined that nobody would steal the months of dedication he had been putting into securing his spot and the aerial space above it.

*Illustration 1.7* Hackers invade the aerial space in Céspedes Park.

How could he explain this to his clients, unhappy about his service? Isaac understood their frustration, some clients were trying to connect to and communicate with family members living abroad. It was a stressful and emotional moment for everybody.

Accompanied by his friend Juan, Isaac walked towards the two men who were already busy responding to a line of potential clients (Illustration 1.8). Isaac confronted one of the hackers, "What's happening man? What are you doing in my territory?" The man responded saying, "Hey my friend, calm down, who says this is yours? I'm just sitting in the park, what's wrong with that?" After a few more exchanges

*Illustration 1.8* Isaac and his business partner confront invading hackers in Céspedes Park.

that were far from friendly, Isaac decided to end the conversation with a clear warning: "You better watch your back, 'cause you're invading my space, and everybody is on my side, you are not welcome here." Isaac knew he could not push it too much, as policemen were everywhere and he did not want to be arrested for disrupting the peace in the park. He was also cautious of the fact that an arrest could bring other problems because of his quasi-illegal business reselling wi-fi signals. Despite the fact that Isaac liked to think about this corner of the park as his own, he knew very well that he was standing in a public space and that he could not always avoid other spatial invasions.

Frustrated, Isaac fantasised about using the wi-fi connection as a weapon to fight the invaders. He once told me jokingly that in trying to protect an invisible signal from potential invaders, he is involved not only in a "wi-fi war" but also in a "star war" (Illustration 1.9). But regardless of his vexation, Isaac did not allow his attention to remain absorbed by the dispute. Despite the stress caused by the presence of the rival hackers in "his" territory, he knew that his services were based on a solid and efficient system and that he had regular clients who had bought his services for months, so he was optimistic that his competitors would not last long. Plus, he was already so busy with all the clients connecting to his wi-fi signal on Mother's Day that he could not lose more time battling with the dark side, at least not today. In addition, Isaac was well aware that his business was ephemeral; it was only a matter of time before more powerful forces would find a way to repress hackers. But for the moment, he felt "the force was with him." Soon after I met Isaac, the police began to target wi-fi resellers. Also, the price of ETECSA access cards went down, which meant that Isaac also had to reduce the cost of his services, diminishing his profit margin. In the

*Illustration 1.9*  Isaac wishes he could use the wi-fi connection as a weapon to fight the invaders.

long run, this discouraged him from continuing with his wi-fi reselling business, and he moved on to focus on using his entrepreneurial talents and tech skills on other services in Cuba's developing market of illegal, quasi-legal, and legal small businesses.

## Conclusion

The composed attitude adopted by Isaac towards the other hackers who invaded his aerial territory and the signals crossing it ironically reminds me of the official ETECSA pay-as-you-go access card. Each card features a photo of a woman sitting in a cross-legged yoga position. Her veins are blue like the colour of her yoga clothes, and she is in deep state of meditation. Behind her, three sketches show her in action: talking on a landline, a cell phone, and working on a laptop. She is in control of her communication. This representation of the services offered by ETECSA contrasts drastically with the experiences most Cubans encounter every day when they communicate by phone (see Chapter 5) and, more recently, when they purchase internet time to connect with their friends and family abroad. If nothing else, the woman meditating in a yoga position on the ETECSA card is a reminder that whilst in Cuba we need to take a big breath every time we wish to access the World Wide Web.

The international wi-fi logo is inspired by the yin-yang symbol (Illustration 1.10), and it emphasises the "Zen" ambiance offered by aerial signs. Wi-fi technology is associated with lightness, playfulness, and mobility. Wi-fi represents a form of freedom from cables and heavy infrastructures of communication. Yet, as we reflect on Isaac's story, we realise that the circulation of those precious signals in the sky is supported by a weighty physical infrastructure, even if we do not notice it. A defective router reminds us that we are dependent on tools and cables to access the web. We might imagine the "cloud" as above our heads, located somewhere in aerial space, but it is in fact constituted by webs of cables, wires, and server farms rooted in our walls,

*Illustration 1.10* The international wi-fi logo.

grounds, landscapes, and aerial spaces. The ingenuity of Cubans to dig into these complex systems, often with little resources and information, to respond to an unreliable infrastructure and to cope with digital scarcity, is laudable. There is, indeed, nothing light about wi-fi signals.

In the next chapter, we shift our attention towards a system used by Cubans to push away non-desired energies coming from envious people. Placed on rooftops, watching the street, cactuses are used to protect households; they are implicated in their own way in the invisible circulation of signals in the Cuban sky.

## Notes

1  On scarcity and invention, see Boudreault-Fournier 2016.
2  ETECSA stands for *Empresa de Telecomunicaciones de Cuba S.A*, and it refers to the Cuban state-owned telecommunication company.
3  For more information, visit https://freedomhouse.org/report/freedom-net/2014/cuba.
4  More details available here: https://freedomhouse.org/report/freedom-net/2018/cuba.
5  On the speed of digital file circulation through memory stick in Cuba, see Cristina Pertierra 2012.
6  For instance, see "SNet, la intranet callejera tolerada por el régimen" published in *Diario de Cuba* on January 27, 2015 by DHCuba. Article available at this address: http://dhcuba.impela.net/2015/01/snet-la-intranet-callejera-tolerada-por-el-regimen/
7  There are also illicit venders who re-sell ETECSA cards in the park for USD 2–3 for one hour of connection, which is more expensive than the service offered by Isaac.

## References

Boudreault-Fournier, Alexandrine. 2016. "The Fortune of Scarcity: Digital Music in Circulation." In *The Routledge Companion to Digital Ethnography*, edited by Larissa Hjorth et al. New York: Routledge, pp. 344–353.
Cristina Pertierra, Anna. 2012. "If They Show Prison Break in the United States on a Wednesday, by Thursday It Is Here: Mobile Media Networks in Twenty-First-Century Cuba." *Television & New Media* 13(5): 399–414.
Leigh-Star, Susan. 1999. "The Ethnography of Infrastructure." *American Behavioural Scientist* 43(3): 377–391.
Recio Silva, Milena. 2014. "La hora de los desconectados. Evaluación del diseño de la política de 'acceso social' al Internet en Cuba en un contexto de cambios Milena." *Crítica y Emancipación* 11: 291–378.
Venegas, Cristina. 2010. *Digital Dilemmas: The State, the Individual, and Digital Media in Cuba*. New Brunswick: Rutgers University Press.

# 2   Cactus

I married the son of Maria Elena on the 3rd of January 2007. This story is about her *lucha*, or "struggle" as they commonly say in Cuba, to build a secure home for her loved ones. I remember when I met Maria Elena for the first time in her home located in the city centre of Santiago de Cuba. She was watching TV in her dark living room, and she did not really acknowledge my presence. A phlegmatic "hola" was the only thing she gave me that evening. Yet, I got to know her little by little when I stayed at her place for more than eight months. Life has not been easy for Maria Elena, although she would never admit it. Born in a family of five children from parents who worked for almost nothing, she was a single mother at the age of 17. She never abandoned the idea of becoming a professional nurse, which she successfully accomplished by age 29. Today, she is the mother of three children, and wife of Edilberto (see Chapter 4), and has had her share of struggles. Yet, the burden of constructing a house for her family is a weight she has carried on her shoulders for decades (Illustration 2.1).

Since the beginning of her adult life, Maria Elena has been passionately struggling to renovate and expand her modest house to accommodate her whole family. Fifteen years ago, her home was a damp single-room shack with only one window that housed five family members. Today, it is a two-bedroom house. However, the house still feels cramped for the family, and it needs a lot of repairs. She has worked hard to build a legacy she wants to leave behind to her children. But taking care of a house is a never-ending process, and she thinks that it is time to continue building. As Maria Elena well knows, undertaking construction in Cuba is far from an easy enterprise.

Housing is a pressing issue in Cuba, and not only for Maria Elena. Many Cubans live with three or four generations sharing the same small residence. The housing shortage has direct consequences on quality of life, as anxiety associated with overcrowding and worry about the

*Illustration 2.1* My mother-in-law Maria Elena.

gradual decay and potential collapse of dwellings takes a toll. Despite the efforts to allocate a house to every Cuban family, the housing projects undertaken by the revolutionary government at the beginning of the 1960s were costly, whilst there was also an urgent necessity to distribute resources to other sectors such as health, education, and dams (Díaz-Briquets 2009). Since the 1970s, it is estimated that thousands of housing units are lost each year because of poor maintenance (Díaz-Briquets 2009:432). With the collapse of Cuban's main trading partner, the Soviet Union at the beginning of the 1990s, the objective of housing all Cuban families has met challenging obstacles. Cement, amongst other things, was severely curtailed during the Special Period, and so were all imports (Díaz-Briquets 2009). Construction materials became difficult if not impossible to find, and the government's priorities turned towards the tourist industry in order to generate revenue. As a consequence, it is almost impossible for most young people in Cuba to think about living in their own house or apartment with a partner and children because there is often nowhere to go—there is no available housing. The scarcity of homes creates distress, psychological problems, and social pressures.

The shortage of construction material is Maria Elena's worst nightmare. Searching for cement bags, *cavillas* (rebar, or steel bars used to reinforce walls and structures), a J-pipe for the kitchen sink, a toilet seat, or a special screw, is her daily routine. Construction materials and supplies have to be found bit by bit, through great effort, sometimes over a long period of time. There are no big hardware stores where one can buy everything needed. All the necessary materials have to be collected in advance and separately (Illustration 2.2). To make matters worse, construction materials remain expensive for most Cubans. Some are only available in stores that sell everything in CUCs, and although other materials are available through the state system in *pesos Cubanos*, which are cheaper but rarely obtainable. Often, tools and construction

*Illustration 2.2* Cement bags stored in Maria Elena's house.

materials are only available on the black market. When Maria Elena finds something she needs, she stores it in the main room of her house. But like anything, materials can be damaged, lost, or stolen.

During a tropical storm, rain seeped into Maria Elena's house and soaked 50 bags of cement that she had bought on the black market just a month prior (Illustration 2.3). It had taken her ten months of sacrifice to raise sufficient money to buy the bags of cement. She was planning to use them for the construction of an extra room. But again, the project would have to wait.

After realising that she lost all of her cement, Maria Elena raised her eyes towards the sky, asking her protector saints to give her the strength to cope with this difficult and stressful situation (Illustration 2.4). All that effort gone with the rain. Without even thinking about it, Maria Elena donned her necklaces and *bandana Africana*, as she commonly calls her kerchief, and, lighting a *tabaco* (cigar), she blew smoke over the construction site.

The necklaces she carefully put on were not just any kind of jewels. They are used to call the saints. These strings of beads are associated with Santería, a Cuban religion of devotion to the African spirits,

*Illustration 2.3* Tropical storm in Santiago de Cuba.

*Illustration 2.4* Maria Elena calling on her saints to ask for strength.

called *orishas*, deities that over time have also come to be associated with Catholic *santos* or saints. The *orishas* are known to possess powers called *aché*. Cuban ethnographer Natalia Bolívar defined an *orisha* as a "pure, immaterial force that is only perceptible to human beings when one of the descendants [practitioner, believer] is chosen by the orisha to be possessed" (1993:137). Santería rituals or *toques* typically involve drumming, chanting, and spirit possession. Each necklace, identified by its coloured beads, corresponds to an *orisha*. For instance, alternate red and white beads represent Shangó, an *orisha* associated with the Catholic Illustration of Saint Barbara, whilst yellow beads are for the African deity Oshún, who is associated with Our Lady of Charity of El Cobre (discussed in the Introduction). Maria Elena decided to wear two necklaces that day: a white one, representing Obatalá, a saint associated with purity and wisdom; and a blue one, representing Yemayá, the saint of the ocean (Maria Elena was chosen by Yemayá to be her spiritual daughter). She believed that the necklaces, and their associated saints, would help her find the strength to move forwards.

Varied religious beliefs exist simultaneously in Cuba, and people associate themselves with different devotions, sometimes at the same time, or they may alternate between them. The religious beliefs under the Afro-Cuban umbrella are complex, in constant change, and cannot be approached as unconnected traditions. These religious beliefs and practices entered Cuba with the thousands of African slaves who were forcibly transported to Cuba between the 16th and 19th centuries as part of the Atlantic slave trade. Most of the indigenous population of Cuba, mainly, Taino, Siboney, and Arawak, died within the first 75 years of contact with the brutality of Spanish colonial domination. Thus, from 1518 onwards, large numbers of Africans were brought to replace the original native population of the island to work as slaves in the sugarcane plantation economy. By two centuries later, in 1814, slaves and free people of African descent comprised 58.6% of the Cuban population (Paquette in Moore 1998:17).

The two most widely known Afro-Cuban religions in Cuba are Santería or Regla de Ocha, and the Regla de Palo or Regla de Congo, better known as Palo. Santería and Palo are so intertwined that it is not productive to look at them as completely separate religions. There are a multitude of intersections between both practices and also with other religious beliefs such as Catholicism and Espiritismo (Spiritism in English, more below). Santería could not have evolved without Palo and vice versa (Palmié 2002). Some *santeros* (priests of the Santería religion) are also *palomeros* (priests of the Palo religion), and believers might opt for one religion or the other depending on which one they think offers the best options for resolving their problems and fulfilling their needs.

Spaniards introduced Catholicism to Cuba at the beginning of the colonial period. Before the Cuban Revolution of 1959 and the government's embarking on a socialist path, the Catholic Church played a role in education and welfare as well as promoting national identity (Crahan 1989). Yet, historian Antoni Kapcia argues that it might be a misleading assumption to think that Cuba was a strong Catholic country for "while the official Church's active base tended to lie in its traditional roots of the white urban middle class, many thousands of

Cubans (mostly, but not all black) described themselves as Catholic but in reality followed *santería"* (Kapcia 2008:146, original emphasis; see also Crahan 1989). Afro-Cuban religions are inclusive and not constrained to one system of beliefs. As a matter of fact, believing in *one* religion is hardly imaginable in the Cuban context.

Espiritismo probably constitutes the most widespread system of beliefs in Cuba, but again, it cannot be approached as completely separate from what today is associated with Santería, Palo, and Catholicism. Spiritism originated as a doctrine imagined by a French founder, Hippolyte Léon Denizard Rivail—also known as Allan Kardec—and spread across the world, including Cuba. By the middle of the 19th century, Espiritismo had become popular amongst the white upper classes in many parts of Latin America. But in Cuba, it rapidly became appropriated and transformed by followers of Afro-Cuban religions. Many Cubans identify themselves with Espiritismo, or with practices embedded within Espiritismo. During a *mesa*—a "mass" or ceremony—practitioners chant and celebrate the presence of the deceased who they believe are watching over and remain part of our living world. Many Spiritists keep pictures of the family dead on a table or shelf along with flowers and bowls of water. A person with abilities to communicate with the departed (in English such a person may be referred to as a "Medium" or "Spirit Medium") may help believers hear advice or blessings directly, or a family may hold a *misa* simply to honour and propitiate those who have passed on.

It is beyond the scope of this chapter to delve into the details of each of these religious practices (and there are others!). Yet, I wish to emphasise that there are no clear-cut boundaries between one religious practice and another. The distinctions between Cuban spiritual devotions are the product of varied historical processes of categorisation and naming that do not necessarily reflect concrete differences (Palmié 2002, 2013). Maria Elena identifies herself with both Catholicism and Espiritismo, but she also integrates practices and beliefs associated with Santería (even if she does not always want to admit it). However, she always dissociates herself from Palo, which she perceives as shadier and malicious. This is indicative not only of the continuous and overlapping nature of the Afro-Cuban religions but also of the political dimensions associated with religious identification in the public sphere.

Despite requesting the help of her saints on multiple occasions, Maria Elena was not at the end of her bad luck (Illustration 2.5). In October 2012, hurricane Sandy destroyed 17m of a newly constructed wall in her home. Sandy was a very strong hurricane, reportedly clocking winds of

*Illustration 2.5* Maria Elena feels hopeless after the hurricane Sandy destroyed a wall of her house.

200 km. In a city with a population of around 500,000, Hurricane Sandy damaged 171,000 homes, of which 22,000 were partially destroyed and 16,000 totally ruined.[1]

Maria Elena felt disheartened. She had no other recourses than to call on her saints again and ask them for help. She threw water, eggshells, and perfume on the floor of the construction site (Illustration 2.6). Unfortunately, these offerings were not enough to reverse her run of bad luck. The normal shortage of construction material intensified after the hurricane because of the high demand for resources to re-build. She could not find anything she needed. There were no pipes for her water system, no cinderblocks, no rebar, no wood… nothing.

After much despair, Maria Elena finally concluded that someone was responsible for her series of misfortunes. There was something peculiar about having to go through so many episodes of bad luck. She could not stop thinking that an envious person had provoked and orchestrated the ruinous events in order to stop her from achieving her goals. What else except the negative force of a jealous and malicious person directed towards her household could explain such a sequence

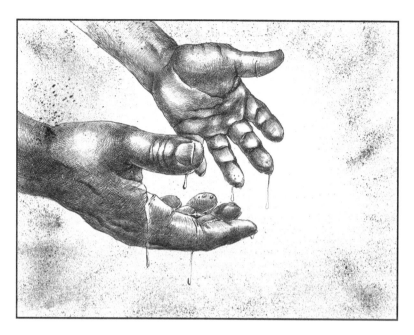

*Illustration 2.6* Maria Elena throws water, eggshells, and perfume on the floor to call her saints.

of bad luck? When there is no explainable cause for the recurrence of bad luck, *mala vista* often becomes a way to make sense of disasters, fights, violence, and loss.

In Cuba, *mala vista*, also called *mal de ojo* (literally "bad sight" and "bad eye" but denoting the "evil eye") refers to a negative wave of energy that affects the life of a person by inciting a sequence of bad luck or misfortunes. The iconography associated with the concept of *mala vista* or *mal de ojo* features an eye with a tongue below it pierced by a dagger and dripping blood (Illustration 2.7). It is a common image that can be seen in many Cuban homes, usually hanging above a doorframe or on the back of a door. The *mal de ojo* talisman is used by Cubans to repel those who might have harmful thoughts or ill intentions that can affect one's well-being. The eye represents a vigilant protector, and the tongue (the *mala lengua*, translated as bad, or evil, tongue) signifies that the icon stops others from talking behind one's back. Finally, the dagger suggests the idea of revenge.

I often heard about fears of the presence of evil eyes or the harmful power of jealousy in Cuba. It is common for Cubans to keep a project

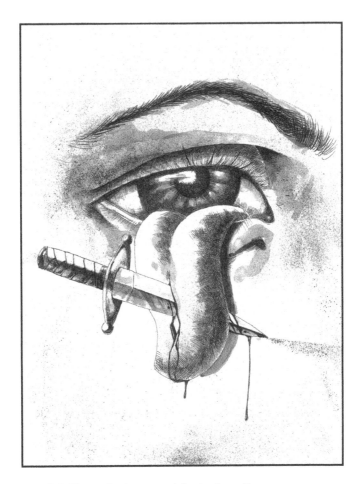

*Illustration 2.7* The *mala visa*, or *mal de ojo*, the evil eye.

secret until it is almost concretised, for fear that someone or something could make it fail. For instance, significant life projects, such as getting married to a foreigner, preparing paperwork to leave the country, or constructing a house, are often kept secret until the last minute. When a friend opens up about an important endeavour, it is not rare to hear something like: "Don't tell this to anybody… because of the *mala vista*, you know, it's better to be cautious." Many believe that a jealous person might make a plan fail due to envious energies.

As well as fear of malevolent energies, many Cubans are also anxious about surveillance or being spied upon, a sentiment that is reinforced by the country's socialist political context. Cubans may alter their behaviour when they talk about a politically sensitive topic in a public space or where they might be heard by people in whom they do not have confidence. In Cuba, *chivatón* is a term that refers to an informer, a rat, or a stool pigeon. Political dissent is tolerated when it is located "within the Revolution," which means that if actions and discourses do not challenge the ideology of the Revolution, then there is place for debate and discussion (Kapcia 2008). However, if someone criticises revolutionary principles, this is usually not tolerated and can be considered counter-revolutionary action or thought. Some people accused of being counter-revolutionary (commonly referred to as *gusanos*, or worms) have left the country, whilst others are in jail. The fear of being heard by someone who could potentially be a *chivatón* is a present concern for Cubans, and this fear resonates with symbols and religious beliefs.

The Cuban Revolution, with Fidel Castro as commander, was already one year old when Maria Elena was born. She has known no other political system or leader during most of her lifetime. Being cautious with whom and how information is shared and keeping things secret until the last minute is part of how she is used to navigating daily life.

Various objects are known to push the evil eye away, and the *ojo de guey* is one of them. The *ojo de guey* is the seed of a plant called *mucuna urens*, about the size of a dice. Cubans often carry this dark brown seed in their pockets or wallets to protect themselves from the *mala vista* when outside their homes. To protect babies and young children, many use a talisman in the shape of a small glass eye that can be tied inside a child's clothing. Maria Elena gave me one when my son Izak was born, and I kept it attached to his pajamas until he was three months old. There are many other examples of amulets or objects that can be used to fend off the evil eye, and I, myself, came to count on them as effective objects of protection.

To protect herself from the *mala vista* of envious people and to reduce the anxiety related to the construction of her house, Maria Elena needed something more powerful than the *ojo de guey*. She decided to call out the big guns and acquire what she considered to be the most potent object to protect her household: a cactus. But not any type of cactus. To effectively "pinch the eyes of jealous people," Maria Elena told me, it had to be a cactus with long, large spines. These spiny cactuses (*Cactaceae opuntia*), called "prickly pear" in English, grow throughout Latin America and the Caribbean. In Cuba, they are commonly known as *tuna*.[2] Interestingly, there is a province in Cuba named Las Tunas, which is located between the provinces of

Camagüey, Holguin, and Bayamo. The *tuna* is a common plant and can be found growing everywhere, but many Cubans told me that the most powerful ones grow in the province of Las Tunas.

I have been interested in the power of the cactus and its spines for a while now, and I had the opportunity to converse about it with a *santera* whom I deeply respect. Her name is Cuca, and she lives in a small city located on the outskirts of Santiago de Cuba called Palma Soriano. During one of my visits to her house, she told me about how the spines of the cactus connect symbolically with the crown of thorns worn by Jesus Christ during his crucifixion. Cuca explained that on the cross, Jesus said, "With the same eyes you look at me, I will look at you. As my eyes are crying, you will cry tears of blood." Although I never found a direct reference to these two sentences in the Bible or in any other documents, Maria Elena also knew about this story when I shared it with her.

Once acquired, the cactus has to be placed on the rooftop or in an elevated position above the home. Maria Elena believes that the cactus acts like a shield for the house and the people who live inside. The cactus, as well as the *mala vista* symbol—which depicts an eye and a tongue punctured by a dagger—and also the thorns worn by Jesus Christ, are assemblages that include pointy objects piercing the human body. In reference to what Cuca had told me about the crown of thorns worn by Jesus Christ, Maria Elena added her own interpretation: "If you do something to me, I'll do it back," adding, "If you envy what I possess or what I do [such as constructing a house], I will pinch your eyes before you can do anything against me."[3] There is a relationship between pointy objects and the idea of reciprocity, revenge, and self-defence represented by thorns, blades, and cactus spines in these assemblages.

Maria Elena is not alone in her belief in the power of cactuses for self-defence. Cactuses placed on rooftops are quite common in Santiago, mainly in the old part of the city where forward-facing rooftops can be observed from the street, and I began to notice them everywhere. In addition to rooftops, people might also hang their cactus on top of their front doorframe or in a window that faces the street. There are no skyscrapers in Santiago de Cuba and very few tall buildings. One can stroll in the hilly streets of the city and see the front of each household. El Tívoli, the neighbourhood where Maria Elena lives, offers an especially rich area to observe the presence of protective cactuses.

Maria Elena first went to a local plant store to find a cactus, but she was not satisfied with any of the ones available. She needed to carefully select the cactus that would protect her household because powerful energies had attacked her. She needed to put a definite end to the *mala vista*. After her disappointing visit to the plant store, Maria Elena decided to take the bull by the horns. She jumped on a truck (a *camión*, a common and cheap means of transportation in rural Cuba) and headed to the province of Las Tunas, a four-hour journey from her home in Santiago, to find the best *tuna*.

Just after arriving in the province of Las Tunas, Maria Elena got off the *camion* and walked around, looking for the best cactus amongst those she saw growing wild along the side of the road. Eventually, she found the perfect one. She opened her arms and embraced the cactus with a sense of love and care (Illustration 2.8). She did not even remember the cactus pricking her, "that's because the cactus was on my side," she said. The cactus will provide protection for her household and allow her to pursue the construction of her house. If necessary, it will even "burst" the eyes of envious people.

When she arrived back home, she planted the cactus in a pot and placed it on the rooftop of her house. She also tied a red cloth to its base. Maria Elena told me that red cloth is associated with Elegguá, the *orisha* that opens doors and paths in life (*abrir el camino*). This deity is understood to dwell "on the very threshold, marking with his

*Illustration 2.8* Maria Elena opens her arms to embrace the cactus.

presence the boundary between two worlds: the inner one of security, and the outer one of danger" (Bolívar 1993:141). In many Cuban spiritual systems, the home is regarded as a haven of security in contrast with the street, which is a place of unexpected and potentially harmful and dangerous energies (Bolívar 1993). The presence of Elegguá, represented by a red cloth, intensifies the power of the cactus in repelling the evil eye, as Elegguá is a protector of the boundaries of the home. Since this deity also facilitates the opening of new paths, opportunities, and possibilities, he is also a sign of hope in the torment of life.

When asked about the power of the cactuses, Cubans commonly explain that the spines of the cactus radiate protective energies outwards, into the sky and surroundings, "pinching the eyes" of the people who might envy them or be jealous of what they possess (Illustration 2.9). When countering *mala vista*, cactuses are the most appropriate and powerful technology of self-defence. Maria Elena, who is still in the process of constructing her house, can now move forward confidently. She has taken all the measures necessary to provide the best protection for her household.

*Illustration 2.9* The spines of the cactus radiate, protecting the household.

## The subtleties of engaging with Afro-Cuban practices visually

The power of the cactus, as shown in the story of Maria Elena, is tied to the beliefs and practices associated with Afro-Cuban religions. The reaction of Maria Elena to one of the drawings made by José Manuel allows for a subtler engagement with these complex connections. The drawing showing Maria Elena's hands dripping with water (Illustration 2.6) has been changed using Photoshop, at her specific request. She did not like the original drawing because of the presence of snails below her hands (Illustration 2.10 is the original version). When José Manuel and I first talked about the drawings that would accompany the story of Maria Elena, we both agreed that this Illustration should depict "Maria Elena calling the saints and spreading water, perfume and eggshells all over the construction site." José Manuel decided to focus on her hands and add the dripping water (often diluted with perfume). In the original drawing, he also decided to include, as part of *his own inspiration*, three snails below her hands, as if she were

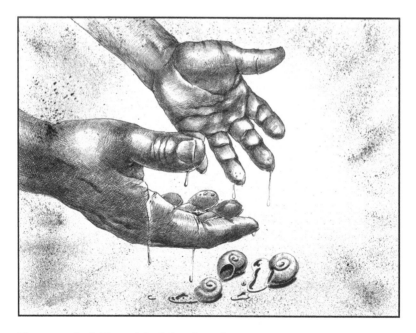

*Illustration 2.10* The original drawing of Maria Elena throwing water, eggshells, and perfume on the floor to call her saints with the presence of three snails.

throwing them on the ground. The position of her hands suggests that the snails had just fallen on the ground. This detail had not attracted my attention. Yet, it was the first thing Maria Elena noticed when I showed her the drawing. She did not like the snails. According to her, they are associated with Santería, a religion she does not identify with fully, at least not openly and publicly.

Maria Elena goes to church every Sunday morning and participates in various trainings, workshops, and activities offered by the local Catholic Church organisation. As mentioned before, she also identifies with Espiritismo and does not see a problem in believing in the two religions simultaneously—Espiritismo and Catholicism—because, according to her, they complement each other. Espiritismo is associated with cleansing, chanting, spirituality, flowers, and good sentiments, and Maria Elena perceives this as a positive spiritual practice. Furthermore, the Catholic Church provides her with the stability of a religious institution and a community of believers and social activities in which she likes to participate, such as singing in the choir and taking part in catechesis discussions offered by the El Cobre congregation.

The snails, in her own understanding of the boundaries between the different Afro-Cuban religions, are associated with Santería, more specifically with divination (forecasting the future), a practice that does not correspond with Espiritismo, nor with Catholicism. Maria Elena strongly emphasised that she is "Catholic" and that she "does not believe in the power of the snails."

Interestingly, José Manuel, who does not share the same perspective and background knowledge of Afro-Cuban religion as Maria Elena, thought that the snails would fit well with her religious beliefs and practices. This is indicative of common forms of imagining and representing Afro-Cuban religions in Cuban popular culture as being divinatory and mysterious. Afro-Cuban religions have been historically associated with *brujería* (sorcery, witchcraft), mainly by the white Cuban population (and sometimes still is today). They were thought of as marginalised social practices, not because a small number of people practised them, but because of their low social status (Wirtz 2004:415).

At the beginning of the 20th century, the Cuban anthropologist Fernando Ortiz wrote a book called *Los negros brujos* (African wizards; 1906 [1995]) in which he explores the religious practices and beliefs of African descendants in Cuba. Associating the religious practices of African descendants with "witchcraft" is indicative of a history of public and scholarly approaches to Afro-Cuban religions that was (and still remains) permeated by racist assumptions (Espirito Santo 2010:67).

Afro-Cuban religions were often associated with superstition and exploitation (Espirito Santo 2010) rather than being understood as complex religions.

At the demand of Maria Elena, we removed the snails from the drawing, but she kindly accepted that I discuss this issue in this book (an issue she would refer to a "mistake"). It is also a reminder that the materiality of religion creates tangible social networks and contributes to the formation of cosmologies that are expressed through various practices that establish boundaries. Maria Elena does not want to be associated with practices she believes are included under the Santería umbrella, or Palo (a religion she totally dissociates herself from because of her negative perception of that belief system).

The fact that Maria Elena defines herself as a strong Catholic, and at the same time believes in the presence of spirits in the human world (Espiritismo), and performs rituals that are associated with Santería (and to a certain extent, one could argue, Palo), shows the extent to which Afro-Cuban religions overlap and mix together. It also illustrates how Cubans select combinations of practices that can help them resolve the particular problems that they face. The conviction that cactuses have the power to push away the evil eye can be located within these complex religious assemblages and networks of beliefs. The snail story suggests that by exploring the significance of certain objects, the ethnographer can engage, albeit indirectly, with the complexity of broader beliefs and practices, encountering Afro-Cuban religions in unexpected ways. Drawings can capture the invisible and the auratic associated with certain items (Taussig 2011:13). In this case, the drawing of the snails created by José Manuel made visible some of the subtleties associated with religious experiences in Cuba. His drawing also provoked a discussion between the anthropologist, the artist, and Maria Elena about the entanglement of religious practices.

## Conclusion

Cactuses are often placed next to analogue TV antennas on Cuban rooftops. Despite being very different, both objects are comprised of one main trunk on which long arms pointing towards the sky are attached. In comparison to TV antennas, whose aim is to receive waves, cactuses are used to push away negative energies. We have seen in the last chapter that wi-fi antennas depend on the electromagnetic fields for the emission of waves through aerial space. Just as analogue TV antennas are technologies of electronic signal reception, and wi-fi antennas transmit radio waves, cactuses are also technologies of self-defence, extending their pointy radiations to prevent the invasion of unwanted forces. Antennas and cactuses are effective technologies of circulation through their respective channels. Rooftops are busy spaces of transmission and reception: they open towards the sky where waves and energies circulate. Both antennas and cactuses are believed to interact with invisible forces, albeit in different ways and through different networks. But all depend on complex infrastructural systems, whether made of cables and wires or religious beliefs. Maria Elena is well aware of this, and she used the means and knowledge at her disposal to most effectively deal with a series of unfortunate events. The next chapter will explore how pigeons, travelling by their own system of orientation, provide another perspective on how things circulate in the sky and how their voyages can reconfigure social, material, and geographic encounters.

## Notes

1 Marc Frank, "Cuban city struggling to recover a year after Hurricane Sandy", Reuters, October 24, 2013. Consulted on April 19, 2016: www.reuters.com/article/us-cuba-hurricanes-idUSBRE99N1G820131024
2 This cactus is called by different names depending on the country. In Mexico, for instance, it is called *nopal*.
3 Interestingly, this interpretation contrasts with what is written in the New Testament, where it is asked to "not resist an evil person. If anyone slaps you on the right cheek, turn to them the other cheek also" (Matthew 5:38–42). I would like to thank Mark McIntyre for bringing this point to my attention.

## References

Bolívar, Natalia. 1993. "The Orishas in Cuba." In *AfroCuba: An Anthology of Cuban Writing on Race, Politics and Culture*, edited by Pedro Perez Sarduy and Jean Stubbs. New York: Ocean Press, pp. 137–145.
Crahan, Margaret E. 1989. "Catholicism in Cuba." *Cuban Studies* 19:3–24.
Díaz-Briquets, Sergio. 2009. "The Enduring Cuban Housing Crisis: The Impact of Hurricanes." In *Cuba in Transition*, paper report from the 2009 Annual Meeting of the Association for the Study. www.ascecuba.org/c/wp-content/uploads/2014/09/v19-diazbriquets.pdf
Espirito Santo, Diana. 2010. "Spiritist Boundary-Work and the Morality of Materiality in Afro-Cuban Religion." *Journal of Material Culture* 15(1):64–82.
Kapcia, Antoni. 2008. *Cuba in Revolution: A History since the Fifties*. London: Reaktion Books.
Moore, Robin D. 1998. *Nationalizing Blackness: Afrocubanismo and Artistic Revolution in Havana, 1920–2940*. Pittsburgh: University of Pittsburgh Press.

Ortiz, Fernando. 1906 [1995]. *Los negros brujos.* Havana: Editorial de Ciencias Sociales.

Palmié, Stephan. 2002. *Wizards and Scientists: Explorations in Afro-Cuban Modernity and Tradition.* Durham: Duke University Press.

Palmié, Stephan. 2013. *The Cooking of History: How Not to Study Afro-Cuban Religion.* Chicago: The University of Chicago Press.

Taussig, Michael. 2011. *I Swear I Saw This: Drawings In Fieldwork Notebooks, Namely My Own.* Chicago: The University of Chicago Press.

Wirtz, Kristina. 2004. "Santeria in Cuban National Consciousness: A Religious Case of the Doble Moral." *The Journal of Latin American Anthropology* 9(2):409–438.

# 3   Pigeon

It took Marlon nine hours by train to arrive in La Florida, a small Cuban town located in Camagüey, one of the central provinces of the island. It was a long journey for a 12 year old boy (Illustration 3.1). Marlon left his hometown of Santiago de Cuba and travelled nearly 340 km. His sole travel companion was his favourite pigeon. Apart from his pigeon, he carried along a few ham sandwiches for the journey. An older lady sitting beside him on the train also kindly shared

*Illustration 3.1* Marlon and his pigeon arrive in the village of La Florida in the province of Camagüey.

her *congrí*[1] and water. The town of La Florida became his destination because it was the farthest place from Santiago to which he could afford to buy a ticket. Marlon had already taken the train a few times to the province of Camagüey with his uncle Edilberto (Chapter 4), and he has cousins who live in Camagüey. But it was not to visit them that he travelled there this time.

A few days before his departure, he told his mother about his intention of travelling to the province of Camagüey to test his pigeon: "Would it be able to fly back home from so far away?" His mother did not give his plan much importance at the time, and she never thought he would really do it. Marlon lives in a single-parent household. His mother works as a civil servant and used to take care of her own mother who was an invalid. Marlon's mother had a lot on her plate and few resources to meet the needs of her family. She works long hours, and because of this, Marlon is extremely mature for his age. He is also a quiet child. Before leaving for the train station, he left a note on the table, telling his mother not to worry, that he would be back the day after, and that he would get in touch with his cousins in Camagüey if he needed help. Marlon works at the *casa particular* (B&B) located across from his house. He serves breakfast to tourists in exchange for a small salary, meals, and gifts from the owner of the business who has taken Marlon under her wings. It is not common for children to work in Cuba, but this is one of the exceptions I witnessed.

Marlon owns many animals—fishes, dogs, and cats—but the ones that really fascinate him are his pigeons. There is something about their intelligence and their ability to recognise the location of their dovecote that really impresses him. Marlon knows about the use of pigeons to carry important messages. Trained from an early age to geo-localise themselves in the sky, pigeons are able to recognise their way back. With small pieces of paper with written information rolled up around their legs, pigeons have transported dispatches *in extremis* during wars. He learned at school that the Cuban national hero Antonio Maceo y Grajales used pigeons in 1895 to carry secret messages to the rebels hidden in the mountains of eastern Cuba during the final war of independence against Spain. Until the 1970s, pigeons were even used in Cuba to transport electoral results from remote areas of the countryside to the city.

There are also impressive reports of pigeons travelling long distances above the ocean. The Brooklyn-based artist Duke Riley spent eight months training 100 pigeons to fly from Havana to Key West, Florida. Half of the birds carried contraband Cuban cigars. The other

half, outfitted with small-scale cameras, documented the 120 km journey across the Strait of Florida. The resulting impressive video footage
shows a top-down view of the birds' journeys. Only 11 out of the 100
made it back home; some arrived in Florida after 5 hours, others took
2 weeks.[2] Riley's project aimed to highlight the long history of smuggling in the Straits, as well as demystifying the cutting-edge technology the national border patrol uses to police what and whom crosses
national boundaries.

All pigeons do not perform such difficult tasks, but "messenger" or
"homing" (*mensejero* in Spanish) breeds were developed centuries ago
through selective reproduction. Apart from carrying letters over long
distances, messengers are also used for racing. In many parts of the
world, pigeon fanciers, or "flyers" (who are mostly men, from teenag-
ers to adults),[3] raise the birds for the love of it and often for the passion
of racing.[4] Cuba is no exception.

In order to train their pigeons for racing, flyers follow a strict series
of exercises. They start by training their messengers daily, typically in
the evening when the heat of the sun is not as threatening. At dusk,
one can witness flocks of pigeons flying in circles over the rooftops
of Santiago de Cuba. When their owners whistle to them, the birds
graciously make their way back to their dovecote. Training also consists of taking caged birds hundreds of kilometres away to let them
practice flying back home. Progressively, the messengers develop the
necessary physical endurance to make longer and longer journeys
back to their dovecote. This is a dangerous sport, as pigeons do get
lost or attacked by predators, and some die of dehydration. Yet, the
risk is worthwhile for many flyers who devote themselves to racing. In
addition to a demanding physical training, serious pigeon breeders
follow a strict and complex diet of dry corn and chickpeas, vitamins,
and minerals.

Marlon started keeping pigeons mainly for pleasure. However, as
his passion grew, he became interested in knowing more about how to
breed pigeons, how to treat their ailments, and how to train them for
racing. He constructed a dovecote on the rooftop of his house using
scrap wood, chicken wire, bricks, and metal sheets (Illustration 3.2).
A stiff ladder, also constructed by Marlon, allowed him to reach the
rooftop from the back interior courtyard of his house. The dovecote
was as tall as he was, with a narrow door that allowed him to enter
and check on his pigeons. Little by little, he accumulated a flock of
25 pigeons. Most were common varieties such as *butchón*, *criolla*, and
*quinterón*, which are part of a flyer's flock but are not trained for racing. He only owned one messenger—his most precious acquisition.

*Illustration 3.2* Marlon at his dovecote on the rooftop of his house.

Marlon received his messenger when it was only a squab (*pitchón* in Spanish), given to him by a neighbour named José Ramón, who is also one of the most famous flyers in Santiago de Cuba (Illustration 3.3). Raising pigeons may seem like a solitary hobby, but it becomes meaningful through the social interactions that it generates (see also Jerolmack 2009, 2013). Flyers need each other to share information, exchange pigeons, and compete in races, amongst other things. José Ramón, who knew Marlon from the neighbourhood since he was a baby, had noticed the boy's dedication to his birds, observing him daily from his own house's rooftop. Having no children of his own and being from an older generation of flyers, he was very sympathetic to a youngster's passion for pigeon-keeping. José Ramón thought that given Marlon's dedication, he was ready for a new challenge.

*Illustration 3.3*  Marlon's messenger pigeon.

The squab became Marlon's most precious companion. Spending long hours on the rooftop of his house to raise the messenger became part of his daily routine (Illustration 3.4). The rooftop became Marlon's refuge, a place where he could hang out in peace, at a distance from all the problems down the ladder.

Walking along the train track after disembarking in La Florida, Marlon remembered the advice given by José Ramón shared with him on the day he brought him the bird: "Love is key, the bird needs to feel loved, to feel well in your house, so that it fights hard to fly back." Despite José Ramón warning that the bird was too young for a 300 km *vuelo de pecho* ("flight of the chest," referring to a long journey), Marlon decided his messenger was ready to be tested. Was he overconfident or stubborn? Was he impatient, or worse, unaware of the dangers? Marlon was determined to let his most precious pigeon try for the seemingly impossible.

Marlon was nervous; his hands were shaking and felt cold despite the tropical weather. He worried, "Will my messenger make its way back home?" The young boy decided to wait a few hours before letting his bird fly and sat below a tree until the sun began slowly making its way down.

*Illustration 3.4* The daily routine of training a pigeon.

Marlon's long journey was not the story of only one day on a train, he had dedicated months of his life to raise his pigeon from a squab to a future champion. Despite his devotion, Marlon remained a young and unexperienced pigeon breeder. He was conscious of this, but he also wanted to impress the older breeders, who were often looking over at his dovecote from their respective rooftops. Marlon wanted to show them that he knew what he was doing. Hopefully, his decision would not cost the life of his messenger.

Many of the older breeders based in Santiago de Cuba are members of a regional group called the National Colombophile Association of Sierra Maestra. Similar pigeon-fancying associations exist all over Cuba. Most notably, the National Colombophile Association

of Havana, founded in 1900—by a young man of only 15 years old—
organised the first long-distance race between Santiago de Cuba and
Havana which covered more than 760 km and took place in 1907
(Bethencourt 2010). These associations are focal points for pigeon
breeders to meet, share information, organise races, and award official recognitions and prizes. Races are held annually with the point
of departure decided by members and transportation provided by the
Association to bring the pigeons to the release destination. Each pigeon is registered with a number that is inscribed on a plastic ring
fixed around the bird's leg. Before the race, the pigeons are weighed
and measured and entered in a catalogue. Then, they are all released
at the same time. Back home in Santiago, the pigeon flyers anxiously
wait for their *protégés* to come back. The first to arrive back to its
dovecote wins the race. Because they each end their journey in distinct dovecotes, it is important to have a system to determine which
pigeon is the winner. To avoid false declarations and cheating, a pigeon flyer will wait for the arrival of another racer's pigeon at the
residence of the other person. Once the pigeon lands (and is identified
by its ring), the breeder in charge calls the Association to register the
pigeon's time of arrival. After phoning, the breeder brings the pigeon
in a cage to the Association within a certain time limit, and the arrival
of the bird is confirmed.

Marlon is not a member of the Association. The annual registration
and competition fees are beyond what he can afford. Marlon also felt
that his pigeon flock was too small and he was too young and inexperienced to become an official member. Maybe one day, he would join
the Association and compete officially with his messenger, but for now
that was not a pressing desire for him. He only wanted to learn to train
a champion, *his* champion.

"You are my favorite pigeon. I believe in you. Fly home and I'll meet
you there.... and be safe..." (Illustration 3.5).

In the flap of a wing, Marlon's messenger was up and away, first in
circling above his head, and after a few minutes, flying towards the
east, which Marlon took as a good sign. Suddenly, Marlon felt lonely
and sad. He gazed at the sky until he could not see his bird anymore,
flying far far away.

Would he ever see his messenger again? Marlon took his empty cage
and made his way back to the station, where he waited for his over-
night train. When he finally arrived back home in Santiago de Cuba
the next morning, the first thing he did was to climb up to the roof of
his house. His messenger was not there, at least not there *yet*. Marlon
was not too worried because he knew that pigeons do not like to fly by

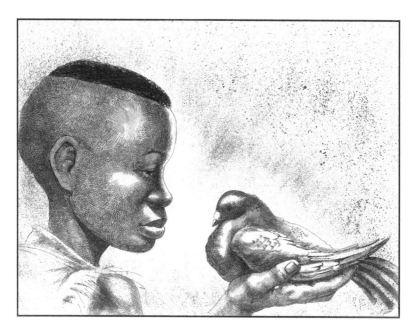

*Illustration 3.5* Marlon talks to his pigeon just before he lets it go. Is this the last time he will see it?

night, so his messenger's journey might well take longer than his train ride. Marlon sat on the roof and looked at the sky, but, tired from his trip, he eventually fell asleep beside his dovecote.

Meanwhile, the messenger was flying towards home (Illustration 3.6). How was it doing it? Nobody really knows, although there are many theories that attempt to explain pigeons' exceptional sense of orientation. In a book about Cuban pigeon-fancying, the author Emilio Bethencourt (2010) discusses three main theories that could explain this phenomenon. The first one argues that the pigeons can find their way back home thanks to the acquisition of a form of landscape recognition acquired through hours of training flying over the dovecote. The second theory is based on the bird's use of the position of the sun and the presence of an internal magnetic field, which would allow the pigeon to orient itself without topographic points of references. The third explanation, which, according to Bethencourt, is unrealistic due to the small size of the pigeon's brain, is a form of complex and adaptable bio-coordinate system based on a highly developed type of long-term memory, which would allow the pigeon to know the exact

*Illustration 3.6* How do pigeons find their way back home from so far away?

geographic position of its dovecote based on the sun at its present zenith location at a specific time of the year. Bethencourt also mentions that in addition, the pigeons might use an internal auditory and/or olfactory type of "card" to orient themselves. The bottom line is that we do not really know.

In a metaphorical way, I can't help but see a connection between the aptitude of the pigeons to find their way back home and the Cubans who leave their homeland in search of a better life elsewhere, and who struggle to come back home to visit their families. Millions of Cubans have left their island since the beginning of the Cuban Revolution in 1959. At first, Cubans left the island because of political reasons, and about 90% of them migrated to the U.S. (Eckstein 2013; Krull 2013). Since the 1990s, after the collapse of Cuba's main trading partner the Soviet Union, many Cubans emigrated to various countries in hope of improving their economic situation as well as helping their family. Most Cubans send remittances home and travel back to visit their family despite economic pressures they encounter in their host country (Eckstein 2013). In a similar way, we could ask if the desire to stay connected with one's home and family is what drives pigeons' journey back home.

*Illustration 3.7* Marlon and his messenger reunited.

At nightfall, Marlon woke up. Before opening his eyes, he heard the cooing of his messenger and the flapping of its wings. Was he still dreaming? Was it his imagination? When he opened his eyes, he saw his messenger. There it was, exhausted and hungry, flying over the dovecote, slowly gliding towards his hand (Illustration 3.7).

## A story about the role of media in cross-cultural collaboration

When José Manuel asked me how we should visually represent the end of Marlon's story, I immediately thought of a frame from the short music video "Pigeon Beats" directed by three of my students who participated in the University of Victoria 2016 Cuba Ethnographic Field School that I organised. As part of the course requirements, students worked in teams to conduct small-scale ethnographic fieldwork with one of the pigeon flyers in my circle of contacts and produce an audio-visual document (soundscape, short film, video, photo essay, etc.) engaging with their research. The three students who worked with Marlon decided to produce a short music video.

In order to fully follow the conversation below, I invite you to watch the music video, which is available online.[5] The last drawing in the story of Marlon (Illustration 3.7) derives from one frame of the video that was filmed and directed by my students (see minute 1:30).

The music video that inspired the drawing allows for a conversation about the potential of visual methodologies to strengthen relationships with participant-collaborators whilst conducting ethnographic fieldwork. Constructing relationships in the field can be quite demanding, and this is often accentuated if there is a language barrier, or when participants do not share the same cultural background, age, nationality, race, or gender (amongst others). None of the three students (all North Americans) directing the music video had an in-depth knowledge of spoken Spanish at the time, and Marlon did not speak English. The three students did not know Marlon prior to the field school, and as mentioned before, Marlon is shy and reserved. During their first meeting, the students climbed up to Marlon's rooftop to see his dovecote and exchanged a few words, looks and laughs with him. But they soon concluded that they needed a better strategy than just hanging out to stimulate fluid and spontaneous conversation with him about his passion. So the students came up with the idea of producing a music video that could showcase Marlon's passion for pigeon-fancying. According to them, a music video produced in collaboration with Marlon would allow for an engaged way to connect not only with his passion for pigeons but also with his interest in music and thus contribute to building a relationship of exchange and conversation. The process of producing the music video would become a way to strengthen their relation with Marlon and to learn about his interests. Also, considering his age and his affinity for local youth popular culture, the young teenager would hopefully be proud to be part of the audio-visual project and, in turn, appropriate it.

The filmmaker and anthropologist Eugenio Giorgianni (2017) explains how making a music video with young musicians living in Goma, Democratic Republic of Congo, generated a common ground that facilitated bonding with the participant-collaborators. In addition to strengthening his relationship with them, crafting the video became a creative way to stimulate a dialogue about the musical ecology of Goma, including the networks of music production, consumption, and dissemination. The production of the music video kindled discussions of topics that were not necessarily sonic nor musical, but other spheres of the social world in which the musicians lived. Working together on a music video became a very effective methodology of research.

After Marlon agreed to collaborate on the production of a music video, they decided that reggaetón—Marlon's favourite—would be the ideal music genre. We contacted Ricardo, a local DJ and producer of reggaetón background tracks, and asked him if he would participate in the project. We introduced Marlon to DJ Ricardo in his recording studio and filmed the visit. DJ producers are highly respected amongst Cuban youth, and this encounter was a significant moment for Marlon. He wore his most stylish clothes for the occasion and got a fresh haircut. In the studio, DJ Ricardo played a few tracks and asked Marlon which one he liked the most. After making his selection, Marlon left the studio with the music track on his memory stick. The students used this track to create a video, meeting with Marlon on several occasions to work on the details. We also asked a local DJ producer and video editor to add visual effects characteristic of the visual aesthetic of the reggaetón music videos that Marlon and most of his friends in Santiago consumed.

An approach to audio-visual methodologies in ethnographic field-work that is sensitive to the visual aesthetics of the people we collaborate with may produce a product that is more meaningful for the collaborator-participants. Everybody, including Marlon (and his mother) was extremely happy with the resulting video, which was presented during a special night-time event in front of the neighbourhood. Also, students gave Marlon a copy of the music video saved on a memory stick.

Let's go back to Illustration 3.7. What captured my attention in this specific frame, and why did I think it could inspire the last drawing for Marlon's story? The position of the video camera, a "low-angle shot" from the ground towards the sky gives the feeling that Marlon is under control, that he is sure of himself. Marlon gazes towards the horizon above the rooftops, then towards the camera located at his feet, and finally sits down with the bird held firmly in his hand. He is proud. It is a beautiful and heartfelt video shot, probably acquired thanks to the relationship that emerged between Marlon and the students. At minute 1:31, Marlon releases his pigeon, and as it flies away, his gaze follows the bird into the horizon. José Manuel and I decided to use the same low-angle empowering perspective to depict Marlon's last visual vignette, so this frame inspired the drawing. However, José Manuel used his artistic freedom to include elements that were not present in the music video still. In the drawing, Marlon's gaze is turned towards his messenger as it lands in his hands with wings still wide open. This contrasts with the video frame in which the bird is about to fly away. The addition or removal of objects in the drawing—making it different from photographs or video clips which may have inspired it—can add layers of interpretation to the story (remember, for example, the snails falling from Maria Elena's hands that are discussed in Chapter 2). The added objects accentuate the material, social, and geographic encounters that were part of the pigeon's journey in the Cuban sky. The two dark lines at the bottom left of the drawing may remind us of electric cables, which hang everywhere over the streets of Santiago. The two lines are in fact clotheslines, placed by Marlon's mother in the tiny interior courtyard where the sun reaches down in the afternoons. Clotheslines are usually made of rope (or, in Cuba, it is not rare to see clothes lines made of old electric cables!). Attached between two points, they can represent a connection between two locations and, in this sense, metaphorically echo the pigeon's journey. A TV antenna placed on Marlon's right side contrasts with the cactus drawn on his left side. The antennas and the cactus remind us of technologies and strategies that attract desired waves or push away unwanted energies (discussed in Chapter 2), as humans try to control the forces of life.

The last drawing of Marlon's story is the product of transforming a moving digital image into a fixed frame, which, in turn, was interpreted and re-imagined by José Manuel into a two-dimensional drawing in black ink on paper. It also indirectly represents a story of efforts to build relationships between anthropologists and collaborator-participants, and which inspired them to create a project that would involve Marlon in the ethnographic process and empower him.

## Conclusion

We are not sure how a pigeon flies back to its dovecote; the bird possesses and uses an as-yet undetermined technology of localisation when moving across landscapes. Rooftops are a place of exchange and encounters, and Marlon too is part of this circulatory system; he raised the pigeon. Maybe the bird returns because it loves its home and feels a connection with Marlon. In this sense, pigeons may not be that different from Cubans living abroad who struggle to visit those they have left behind on the island. Indeed, we might believe, as do some pigeon fanciers from Santiago de Cuba, that love is the fuel that drives the pigeon back home as it struggles against the many obstacles present in the Cuban sky.

In a soundscape project produced by three other students also participating in the University of Victoria 2016 Cuba Ethnographic Field School, we can hear the pigeon fancier Ernesto Martín Garcés from Santiago de Cuba saying, "The pigeon returns home because it loves its home. It is treated well. [...] They are my daughters. I love them with my heart and soul."[6] The strong attachment of pigeon fanciers to their birds (and vice versa) works as an anchor point at the end of the long journey. If not, what other forces would be robust enough to drive them back? The feminist theorist Donna Haraway (2016) writes that we need to look at the pigeon-human relationship (and other multispecies connections) as being constituted by each other, what she refers to as the "becoming-with." The pigeon is trained to come back to its dovecote, and the pigeon fancier becomes adept at training pigeons thanks to love and dedication. A two-way connection takes place, a form of active reciprocity that alters the two protagonists along the way (Haraway 2016). This mutual force that constitutes the "becoming-with" encapsulates the process that taught Marlon how to love and to care for another species. It also helps us imagine why the pigeon makes its way back home.

In the next chapter, we broaden the skies above Santiago de Cuba to a larger territory. In thinking about chance and the lottery, we observe the course of winning numbers that travel in a cosmic space, above national and translational lands and oceans, and examine the hopes and fates of players who gamble on faith.

## Notes

1 Rice with beans.
2 See "Avian Artistry, With Smuggled Cigars" by Melena Ryzik in the *New York Times*, October 16, 2013 (www.nytimes.com/2013/10/17/arts/design/avian-artistry-with-smuggled-cigars.html). For more details and to watch the footage, see the artist's website: www.dukeriley.info/trading-with-the-enemy/. Duke Riley has also created other art projects with pigeons: in "Fly By Night" he equipped birds with small LED beams and sent them into the sky at night for a spectacular light show (www.youtube.com/watch?v=QSQn2oXzBXo).
3 I have never met a woman who raises pigeons, and none of the flyers I met in Cuba knew of any. Female partners of flyers I met all revealed that they had to be patient with their husband as they spent more time on the roof than helping them with the household chores. Many women humorously reported having felt jealousy for the pigeons. "But at the end of the day" Noa, the wife of a flyer told me, "I prefer my husband on my roof than hanging out I don't know where with some pigeons (*paloma* – meaning women) out there!"
4 For instance, in New York (Jerolmack 2009), Italy (Jerolmack 2009, 2013), California (Haraway 2016), and France (Despret 2013).
5 The music video clip, directed by Dazzle Krasle, Hilary Morgan Leathem, and John McIver, is available at https://vimeo.com/181731542. The Sonoptica Vimeo page (https://vimeo.com/user51020100) collects videos and film projects produced by the students of the Anthropology Department at the University of Victoria. The other Cuba Ethnographic Field School 2016 projects are posted on the Sonoptica Vimeo page.
6 The soundscape produced by Aviva Lessard, Diane Schimpl, and Lydia Toorenburgh is available on the Sonoptica Vimeo page: https://vimeo.com/178772435.

## References

Bethencourt, Emilio. 2010. *La colombofilia en Cuba*. La Habana: Publicaciones de la Oficina del Historiador de la Ciudad de La Habana.

Despret, Vinciane. 2013. "Ceux qui insistent. Les nouveaux commanditaires." In *Faire art comme on fait société – Les nouveaux commanditaires*, edited by Didier Debaise, Xavier Douroux, Christian Joschkey, Anne Pontégnie and Katrin Solhdju. Paris: Les presses du réel, pp. 133–146.

Eckstein, Susan. 2013. "Cubans without Borders: From the Buildup to the Breakdown of a Socially Constructed Wall Across the Florida Straits." In *Cuba in a Global Context: International Relations, Internationalism, and Transnationalism*, edited by Catherine Krull. Florida: University Press of Florida, pp. 287–301.

Giorgianni, Eugenio. 2017. "Collaborative Music Video Making in the CityScape of Goma (RDC) #VISUALANTH." *Allegralab*, April 24. http://allegrala boratory.net/participatory-camera-as-a-gatekeeper-collaborative-music-video-making-in-the-cityscape-of-goma-the-democratic-republic-of-the-congo/

Haraway, Donna J. 2016. *Staying with the Trouble: Making Kin in the Chthulucene*. Durham: Duke University Press.

Jerolmack, Colin. 2009. "Primary Groups and Cosmopolitan Ties: The Rooftop Pigeons Flyers of New York City." *Ethnography* 19(4):453–457.

Jerolmack, Colin. 2013. *The Global Pigeon*. Chicago: The University of Chicago Press.

Krull, Catherine. 2013. "Introduction: Cuba in a Global Context." In *Cuba in a Global Context: International Relations, Internationalism, and Transnationalism*, edited by Catherine Krull. Florida: University Press of Florida, pp. 1–24.

# 4  Lottery

Sitting on his front porch, Edilberto watched passersby leisurely making their way back home whilst chatting with friends and family. In the evenings, the streets of Santiago come alive with neighbours trying to catch a fresh breeze and escape the heat accumulated inside their homes. It is common for people to bring their chairs out to their front porch, the sidewalk, or literally, into the street, to relax and chat with neighbours and watch their young children play. In his early 70s, Edilberto, whose nickname is "el Morro," was taking a few minutes to relax with a filterless *criolla* cigarette clasped between his lips. Edilberto owns a small business; he has a fruit and vegetable stand at the market called La Plaza located near the old port in the city centre of Santiago de Cuba. Despite his age, Edilberto is still working hard. The retirement pension offered by the Cuban government—about USD 8 per month—does not cover his expenses. So he wakes up at 4:00 AM every day, except Mondays, to buy fresh seasonal merchandise from local producers to sell at his stand. He likes his work; the effervescence of the market is now part of his daily routine and keeps him spry and engaged. He is also very good at what he does, he knows the business and how to maximise his profitability.

Edilberto is my father-in-law and a sweet and caring person. He is generous with his children and friends. In good faith, he gave me a piglet for my previous birthday, which I kindly accepted on the condition that he raises it on my behalf (having nowhere to leave it in Cuba, and surprisingly for Edilberto, not being allowed to carry it back with me on the plane to Canada). After arriving home from the market at the end of the workday, Edilberto used to ask me to count his profits for him. In silence, he would hand me a stack of Cuban pesos whilst I watched television and would wait for me to tell him his daily gain. I have to admit that I enjoyed those moments: I could tell he was proud of showing me his profits—I am his daughter-in-law, but I am also a foreign woman from a rich country. Maybe it was a way for him to validate that he is a successful businessman, that he knows how to make money (and this is no small thing in a socialist country).

Edilberto was caught up in his thoughts when an old friend came to greet him. Whilst shaking his hand, the old man asked, "Morro, what came out today, any chance?" Edilberto knew that his friend was asking about the results of the *bolita*, a term that means "small ball" and which refers to the illicit lottery system played in Cuba. "I'll go check later, but this one is mine!" responded Edilberto with the hint of a smile. Laughing, the old man continued on his way down the street waving at Edilberto from behind. The results of the winning numbers would be announced later that evening, at exactly 8 PM. Edilberto is not a regular gambler, but he likes to bet once in a while. Gambling is everywhere in Cuba; some like betting on animal fights—bulldogs, cocks, and betta fishes—others prefer wagering on dominoes, baseball, and, more recently, soccer. Edilberto has a weakness for the *bolita*. He promised Maria Elena (his wife, and my mother-in-law; see Chapter 2) that he would not spend any of the money dedicated to household expenses to play *bolita*, but sometimes the temptation is too strong. Edilberto was convinced that this time he had picked winning lottery numbers. Why was he so sure about it *this* time? In order to answer this question, we need to consider some aspects of Cuban gambling.

Edilberto was 13 years old in 1959 at the beginning of the Cuban Revolution. He remembers the *barbudos* (bearded men, referring to the *guerilleros*, the armed revolutionaries) glamorously entering Santiago de Cuba. Their charismatic commander Fidel Castro declared the triumph of the Cuban Revolution from the balcony of the City Hall, located just three streets from the house where Edilberto and his family still live today. Before the Revolution, the lottery system was legal, and Edilberto remembers—although he was very young—that he enjoyed playing *bolita* once in a while. Many casinos and gambling houses also operated in Cuba's capital, Havana. And, closer to Santiago de Cuba, in the city of Guantánamo, American tourists and servicemen from the U.S. army base there spent money and gambled in the various entertainment venues available during the pre-revolutionary era. At that time, many of Cuba's casino businesses were owned by the mafia. Fulgencio Batista's dictatorship (the elected President of Cuba from 1940 to 1945, he ruled again as the U.S.-backed authoritarian ruler from 1952 to 1959, until he was overthrown by Fidel Castro) tolerated prostitution and other illegal activities. Gambling, and more specifically the lottery system, had long existed in Cuba. The Spanish colonial government legalised gambling and established the national lottery in 1812. Evidence suggests that gambling was widespread amongst all social classes (Sáenz Rovner 2008). Esteban Montejo, a former slave whose life story was chronicled by the Cuban anthropologist Miguel Barnet (1994), recounted various forms of gaming and betting taking place on the sugar plantations. In referring to gambling, the Cuban critic, essayist, and anthropologist José Antonio Saco (1946:30) wrote that in the 19th century (when Cuba was still a colony of Spain), there "was no city, village, or corner of the island of Cuba into which this all-consuming cancer has not spread."

But the lottery, casinos, entertainments, and prostitution did not correspond to the new ideal socialist society Fidel Castro and his *guerilleros* aimed to establish. Just one month after the fall of Batista and the triumph of the Revolution, Castro's new regime decided to supress the national lottery, which he considered a social parasite and a source of political corruption and immorality. Next, Castro prohibited cockfights, and a few years later, the regime closed all casinos, gambling institutions, and brothels. Elders in Santiago de Cuba told me that after the Revolution, the *bolita* was persecuted and later tolerated as the government focused on other social advances, but it never disappeared completely as an entertainment amongst the population. Today, the *bolita* is still illegal but widespread, and its infrastructure is based on an effective and secret pyramidal network.

Earlier the same day, Edilberto had a powerful dream during his daily afternoon nap, the type of dream that stays alive when you wake up, that leaves a mark. In this dream, he was in the middle of an empty field and a young dashing horse was galloping around him and whinnying, as if it wanted to warn him of something (Illustration 4.1). Edilberto was not afraid, he felt connected to the horse. He could tell the animal knew something and that it was important. But he did not know what the horse had to tell him, at least, not yet.

On his way back to the market to finish his workday, Edilberto took his cart by the house of a local middleman to pick up a bag of potatoes. He also stopped at the local state-owned butcher shop to collect his family's monthly share of eggs.[1] This was not his usual route to the market, but this afternoon, he felt he had to "borrow this path." At the corner of Santa Rita and Padre Pico streets, in a small adjacent square, he noticed a horse, strikingly similar to the one he just dreamed about (Illustration 4.2). It was not that unusual to see horses in this area. Street venders often use horse carriages to transport and sell their merchandise in the streets. In Cuba, merchants who sing

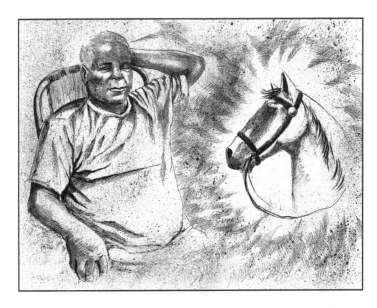

*Illustration 4.1* During his daily afternoon nap, Edilberto dreams of a dashing young horse.

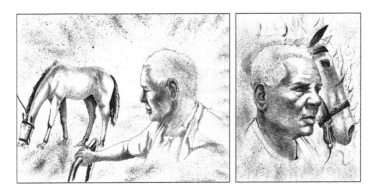

*Illustration 4.2* Edilberto sees a horse at a few blocks from his home. This is a sign that it is time to play *bolita*.

and use their voices in colourful ways to sell their wares are known as *pregoneros* (see Chapter 5). In fact, the owner of the horse had a cart full of mangoes and were just pausing as the horse was eating a clump of grass. When Edilberto approached the horse, the animal reacted vividly and began to raise its head and scratch the soil with his hoof.

Surprised, but not afraid, Edilberto thought that the coincidence was too strong to ignore. He had just dreamed about a dashing colt, and a few blocks from his house, another horse tried to warn him of something. Edilberto saw this as a sign, a *cábala*. It was time for him to play *bolita*!

A *cábala* (a symbol, or revelation) is a term used to refer to everyday events, objects, and people that in one way or another grab enough attention to warrant a bet. They can be related to a dream, superstitions, or a repetition of appearances during someone's normal daily activities that seem coincidental but are communicative of a cosmic revelation (Holbraad 2010). The presence of a dashing horse appeared to Edilberto as a noteworthy coincidence, thus a *cábala*.

Many Cubans use revelations or *cábalas* to identify the numbers to play *bolita* (more below on the rules of the game itself). Once a player recognises that they have had a *cábala* (a revelation), they find the associated numbers according to a list known as the *charada* (charade). This list includes numbers from 1 to 100 with each number being associated with one or multiple *cábalas*. The lottery system based on the *charada* entered the island with Chinese migrants who came to Cuba to work as indentured labourers on the construction of the railroad that crosses the island (Ortiz and Fernández Robaina in Sáenz Rovner 2008:85). The *charada* consisted of a list of 36 numbers with their associated symbols. Cubans increased the list to 100 and added symbols to the Chinese *charade*. Table 4.1 presents an excerpt from a basic version of the *charada* for numbers from 1 to 20 (the Chinese symbols are in bold).[2]

There is no official and standardised *charada* all over Cuba. Those who play often have photocopied renderings collected in a folder and share these amongst themselves. Most importantly, the *charada* is painstakingly used to decide exactly which numbers should be played. Whilst

*Table 4.1 Charada* for numbers from 1 to 20

| | |
|---|---|
| 1 **Horse**, sun, inkwell [Fidel Castro] | 11 **Rooster** |
| 2 **Butterfly**, man, coffee maker | 12 **Saint woman**, comet |
| 3 **Sailor**, child, cup | 13 **Peacock**, tall child |
| 4 **Cat**, mouth, tooth, key, candle | 14 **Cemetery**, tiger cat |
| 5 **Nun**, sea, padlock | 15 **Dog**, good looking girl |
| 6 **Tortoise**, glare | 16 **Bull** |
| 7 **Shell**, shit | 17 **Moon**, Saint Lázaro |
| 8 **Death**, pumpkin | 18 **Small fish**, palm tree |
| 9 **Elephant**, tongue | 19 **Worm**, flag |
| 10 **Big fish**, president, mesh | 20 **Bedpan** |

there is no official list and there are many versions of the *charada*, the basic symbols and numbers associated with the Chinese *charada* tend to remain consistent. What differs considerably from one version to another are the additional *cábalas* associated with the numbers (examples 1–20 above, not bolded), and all the other *cábalas* and their associated numbers on the list up to 100. There are, therefore, thousands of slightly different versions circulating amongst gamblers. Some versions of the *charada* associate many symbols with one number, whilst others remain simple (only one or two *cábalas* or revelations per number).[3] Some revelations or *cábalas* and their corresponding numbers are common knowledge amongst the population, but are never written down. The most striking example is Fidel Castro. He is associated with the number 1 (also a horse), number 61 (a big horse), and number 45 (the president). Most *bolita* players know this even though the name of the deceased Commander in Chief never appears on a *charada*. It is reported that after the death of Fidel Castro on November 25, 2016, there was a record number of *bolita*[4] bets played that were numbers associated with him. This suggests that gamblers can use political events and news as revelations. They can find inspiration in politics, as well as in dreams and/or in relation with their daily life activities.

If a player does not encounter any event that warrants a bet, it is still possible to find a revelation using the services of a professional diviner or spiritualist who specialises in the drafting of daily *cábala*. These diviners usually sell *cábalas* in the street for the price of one Cuban peso each. The *cábala* sold by diviners consists of a small piece of paper on which is written the day of the week and a riddle with three numbers. I transcribe below two examples of *cábalas* sold by a *bolita* diviner in the Tivolí neighbourhood in Santiago de Cuba.

**Monday**
Number that discusses the most water, and the drunk man →
39-14-85, and take it, it's going away from you.[5]

**Tuesday**
Number that we look for to do witchcraft, and the pigeon →
49–53–80, and take it, it's going away from you.[6]

Gamblers might purchase a *cábala* sold by a diviner and bet on the three numbers written down on the piece of paper. They can also find inspiration from what is written on the paper using their *charada*, or an index to decipher other numbers. In addition to the faith they put into a *cábala*, many Cubans also trust statistics to find out which numbers are most often drawn versus which ones are less likely. It is not rare for regular players to combine the two strategies (*cábalas* and statistics) to increase their chances of winning. However, rationally, the *bolita* is supposed to be a basic lottery game based on the drawing of three winning numbers ranging from 1 to 100. But there are different types of number combinations one can bet on, and it can quickly become complex. The description of the *bolita* betting options collected by anthropologist Martin Holbraad (2010:79) translates the intricacy of the game. I am in part reproducing his description below. In Table 4.2, if a gambler bets 20 Cuban pesos on a number that is first on his list, and that same number is drawn, also in first position (*fijo*), then he can win between 1,200 and 1,500 Cuban pesos, which is a considerable amount (approximately between USD 48 and 60).

After Edilberto witnessed the second horse scratching the soil of the small square, he was convinced that he had just witnessed a powerful *cábala*. It was a special revelation because his dream coincided perfectly with a subsequent event a few blocks from his home. In addition, he never usually takes this road to go to work, a last-minute decision brought him to walk beside the small square. It was as if a cosmic message had been put in place for him to catch. As soon as he arrived at the market, he left his load of potatoes with his assistant Marco (older brother of Marlon; see Chapter 3). Edilberto went straight to Carmen, a vender of spices and aromatic leaves. Carmen, whose stand is located at the back of the market, also collects numbers to play *bolita*. Because the *bolita* remains an illegal game, Carmen's gambling business is not openly discussed and advertised, although all the workers in the market know about it. In Cuba, locations where one can buy a lottery

*Table 4.2* Betting options at the *bolita*

| Type of bets | Structure | Return per bet of one peso (varies in different region of the island) |
|---|---|---|
| Fijo | On first number: **xx** xx xx | 60–75 |
| Corrido | On second or third number: xx **xx** xx or xx xx **xx** | 20–25 |
| Centena | On the last three digits: xx **xx xx** | 300 |
| Parlé | Any two of three numbers in either order: **xx xx** xx, **xx** xx **xx**, or xx **xx xx** | 800–900 |

Source: Based on Martin Holbraad (2010:70) and adjusted according to my own fieldwork in Santiago de Cuba in 2015–2018.

ticket and/or bet on the *bolita* are not obvious. There are no advertisements or signs announcing the sale of lottery tickets. Playing *bolita* is a clandestine activity, and one needs to know through word of mouth where to place bets for the *bolita* with *listeros* (list-keepers).

When Carmen saw Edilberto walking towards her with conviction, she knew he was not there to buy cumin, and asked "What are you going to take today Morro?" Edilberto responded in a decided voice that he would put 500 Cuban pesos on each of the following numbers: 01-50-61 (for a total of 1,500 Cuban pesos; approximately USD 55). The 01 corresponds to the horse, 50 to the mango (there were many in the cart beside the second horse he saw), and 61 is another number for the horse. Carmen looked at Edilberto with surprise. She took a few seconds to write down his bet, as she needed extra time to process the information. This was an enormous bet, probably the biggest she had for months. Edilberto handed her a big stack of money. She took the money, placed it in her bra, and finished writing down the numbers and his name on the *bolita* list for that day. The winning combinations would be announced at 8 PM that same night. There are two draws of the *bolita* each day, with winning numbers announced at 2 PM and 8 PM, but Edilberto never plays the early round, he prefers the evening game.

Carmen is part of a chain of intermediaries that make up the *bolita* infrastructure. She is in the most vulnerable position of various mediators because people know about her business, and *chivatones* (informers; see Chapter 2) could denounce her activities to the authorities. The *mensajero* (messenger) is the next protagonist in line. Their role consists of collecting the lists of bets from the *listeros* and the corresponding money they collected and delivering everything to the head of the structure, the *banquero* (banker) before 8 PM, when the winning numbers are announced (see Table 4.3). All the bets need to

*Table 4.3* The pyramidal infrastructure of the *bolita*

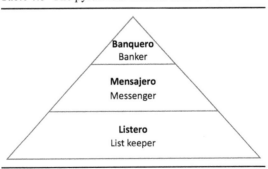

be at the *banquero's* place before that time. If not, the *mensajero* will be responsible for paying the winners, because the *banquero* will not take responsibly for any bets that are reported too late. The *banquero* sits at the top of the pyramid and guarantees the redistribution of the money to the winners through the mediation of the *mensajero* and *listero*. The *banqueros* are the ones who benefit the most from the *bolita* business: the *listeros* and the *mensajeros* are paid only a percentage of the daily collected bets. Various *mensajeros* can work for one *banquero*. Nobody (except the *mensajeros*) know the identity of the *banqueros* or how much they earn—this is kept extremely secret.

Whilst *listeros* might be the most vulnerable agents in the *bolita* infrastructure, because the *banqueros* are the head of the structure, they risk more if they get caught. A *banquero* (and close associates) risk fines and jail sentences for a period of three to eight years if they get caught by the authorities.[7] It is reported that in the city of Santiago de Cuba alone, there are approximately five *banqueros* each with a pyramidal structure operating the *bolita* on a daily basis, but again, we do not know for sure because very few people can identify them. Players only know the identity of the *listero* with whom they deal.

The *banquero* pyramidal structure is a local organisation that is reproduced everywhere on the island. It has its own internal rules (although *banqueros* tend to follow similar regulations nationally). Winning numbers are announced at the national level. This means that there are only one set of winning numbers for the whole country, which is adhered to by all *banqueros*, and as mentioned before, numbers are announced two times per day.

Currently drawn in Miami, *bolita* results are transmitted through three main channels, all of them travelling through aerial spaces. The first and most common way of charting the numbers is by listening to the radio programme "La Poderosa" transmitted by "Radio Martí" based in the U.S.A (Illustration 4.3).

Radio Martí was initiated by the Ronald Reagan administration in the 1980s with the goal of countering Communism by providing propaganda information against the Castro regime to Cubans living on the island. Cuba responded to this ideological attack by broadcasting interference against the radio station, creating radio wars (Frederick 1986; Bronfman 2016) that prevented the programme from being heard on the island. "Radio Martí" comes from the name of the Cuban national hero José Martí who fought against Spanish colonialism and American imperialism in Latin America in the late 1800s. From the Cuban state perspective, it is a political affront for a U.S.-based radio station to broadcast the winning *bolita* numbers in Cuba, an activity

*Illustration 4.3*  The VEF, an old Russian radio.

that remains illegal on the island's national territory. In Cuba, Radio Martí is currently only accessible with a portable short-wave radio. Although I never have been able to catch Radio Martí in Santiago de Cuba, gamblers told me that they are able to listen to this radio station with an old brand Russian radio called VEF, common on the island in the 1960s–1980s, but currently more difficult to find.

The second way of determining the *bolita* numbers is through TV programmes broadcast from Miami and transmitted to Havana via illicit satellite antennas, which are common in Havana but have not yet penetrated Eastern Cuba. Phone calls from Havana inform people in Eastern Cuba of the *bolita* results. The third and more recent way to access the numbers is through an Android phone application called Lucky Strike. Cubans can buy the application via the weekly *paquete* (see Chapter 1). For USD 5 per month or USD 7 for life, Cubans receive the daily numbers automatically via their phone as well as statistics they can use for betting.[8]

*Bolita* players I talked to in Santiago de Cuba are convinced that since the beginning of the 2000s, *banqueros* rely on the *bolita* numbers announced by Radio Martí. But it has not always been so. Before the 2000s, winning numbers used to be announced by Radio Rumbo and

*Illustration 4.4* Edilberto's mind going in all directions.

Ecos del Torbe, two radio stations based in Venezuela. At the time, the *bolita* in Santiago de Cuba was based on a lottery system from Venezuela known as *del Táchira*. It is reported that Venezuelan radio stations stopped broadcasting *bolita* numbers in Cuba after Hugo Chávez (a supporter of Fidel Castro) was elected as the president of that country in 1999.

Edilberto decided to go to bed early at 7 PM. Even though he did not yet know the results, he declared he was confident enough to wait until the morning. But although he did not want to admit it, he was actually nervous and having a difficult time managing his emotions. His mind was going in all directions, thinking about numbers and all the things he could purchase if at least two of his numbers were selected (Illustration 4.4). If he had a *parlé* (two subsequent numbers), he could win more than 320,000 Cuban pesos, and he was thinking of all the things he could finally acquire, including a television set for his bedroom and a new refrigerator.

And what about the motorcycle he saw for sale the other day (Illustration 4.5)! If he had better transportation, he could visit producers outside the city and deal directly with them, thus negotiating better deals for his fruit and vegetable stand in the market. It would

*Illustration 4.5* Edilberto imagines owning a motorcycle.

make his life so much easier. All these possibilities excited Edilberto. But at the same time, he felt exhausted by so many numbers and thoughts floating in his mind. He needed to calm down and take a break. Tomorrow would be another day, a new beginning.

When Edilberto woke up, his confidence was not as strong as the evening before (Illustration 4.6). What if he lost all of his money? Without waiting, he left his home for the market. On the way, he met his co-worker Ramón, and Edilberto asked him, "Do you know what

*Illustration 4.6* The morning after, Edilberto loses his confidence.

came out last night?" With a sleepy voice, Ramón answered that he did not know. When Edilberto finally arrived at the market, he saw his friend Margarita, and he asked her the same question. She replied that she did not know about all numbers but "that the moon came out first." Edilberto felt his heartbeat in his ears and his throat turned dry like sandpaper. Carmen, the *listero* based at the market, was already at her stand chatting with other *bolita* players. They were talking about the moon and the rat, but nothing about the horse. When Edilberto asked Carmen what numbers came out, she confirmed the moon (17), the snow (62), and the rat (29). Hearing the winning *cábalas* fell like a thunderclap, and Edilberto was paralysed.

Edilberto is like any other *bolita* player, with days of luck or misfortune. Dreams, statistics, intuition, superstition, and illusion motivate the *bolita* gamblers, and this is also true for Edilberto. He knows very well that revelations are not fixed in stone. "Sometimes, you think you had a revelation, but it might not be, and you might misinterpret the meaning of a *cábala*," Edilberto told me once. In retrospect, Edilberto is able to reflect on this unfortunate event in a detached way. He knows revelations do not always expose the *bolita* winning numbers. But at the end of the day, this is what makes the game so exciting. Edilberto's unlucky experience did not stop him from gambling. After a few weeks, he was once again caught up in the heat of the game. Being alert to everyday events, dreams, and people he meets, Edilberto is always receptive to *cábalas* that could help him win the *bolita*. With *mente positiva* (positive mind), as Cubans often say, anything can happen, but one needs to be receptive to the revelations that everyday life puts into your way.

## Conclusion

The Cuban expression "When you look at the sky, there is more than meets the eye" offers meaning when we reflect on the story of Edilberto. There are two invisible systems of circulation that take place as the winning numbers of the *bolita* make their way towards Santiago de Cuba. The first one involves the waves that travel in the aerial space that transports information. In this case, the voice transmitted by the radio, announcing the winning numbers. Radio waves travel through a frequency that ranges from 30 kHz (long-wave) up to 3,000 kHz (short-wave) transmitted through a complex field of waves that move in the aerial space surrounding all of us. Other systems of information and energies are transmitted through an electromagnetic spectrum depending on the frequency, such as electric waves, infrared, visible light, x-rays, gamma rays, and cosmic rays. Edilberto's story illustrates that the results of the *bolita* travel through radio, satellites, and Android phones, all technologies that depend on electromagnetic waves. The aerial space in which all of this information travels is actual and physical even if we cannot detect it through our senses. These waves, calculated in Hertz, are part of our daily lives. Our bodies swim in an ocean of waves and energies that cruise along, often invisibly, in a space Anthony Dunne (2005) refers to as the "Hertzian space."

How can waves that we cannot sense affect us? We don't really know. Recently, there have been allegations of sonic attacks on members of the U.S. and Canadian embassies in Havana, an issue that remains unresolved. It is reported that American diplomats suffered from headaches, dizziness, and other perplexing symptoms causing pain and partial deafness. These symptoms are said to be the consequences of mysterious "sonic attacks."[9] Electromagnetic waves can be used to transmit information, they can serve as ideological weapons in the territory of the enemy, and they can also hurt people.[10] Even if the circulation of certain waves can be politically charged and potentially controlled and censured, as shown by the Radio Martí example mentioned earlier, they use the aerial space that surround us to transmit many kinds of information. Thinking in terms of Hertzian space pushes us to reflect on how various fields of energies are interconnected—such as radio, wi-fi, and x-rays—rather than discrete elements. It forces us to think about the electric objects—a phone, a portable radio, a computer—as catalysts that allow the visualisation of those fields of transmission to emerge (Dunne 2005). Finally, it brings us to question how these technologies function and how they are sustained by an infrastructure that is often perceived as invisible, as if these systems of transmission and energy just happen magically.

The second type of circulation in the story of Edilberto is the *cábala* system. Martin Holbraad writes that the *cábalas* "turn on the idea that it is possible to apprehend the cosmos as such" and that the gambler "allows coincidences to suggest themselves to him" (Holbraad 2010:81). The revelations that appear in the everyday life of gamblers are conceived as travelling through the cosmos. Even in its more metaphysical definition, the idea of cosmos is imagined as an abstract and faraway place that is most likely located above our head and probably above the sky. The gambler channels cosmic revelations and translates them into *cábalas* that can be subsequently deciphered through the *charada* (Holbraad 2010:83). As we have seen with Edilberto, the appearance of a horse in his dream, and then seeing a horse close to his home, spoke to him, and he decided to play *bolita* accordingly. Such revelations are available in the gambler's everyday life, one just needs to be receptive and catch the messages as they pass. In the next chapter, sound is at the centre of the story. But this time, it is transported through the instruments of conga players and voices of Cubans wandering in the streets. The sound of the conga bouncing fiercely on the walls of the houses reaches the rooftops with passion.

## Notes

1 The Cuban government distributes a series of subsidised products, via a *libreta* (a ration booklet), to the population at a very low cost. Each member of a family registered at a specific address has the right to a certain number of rationed products, which have varied through the different periods of the Revolution. At the time of writing this book, the Cuban state distributes five eggs per person per month through the *libreta*.

2 Martin Holbraad (2010) also provides the *charada* of 100 numbers and their associated symbols.

3 Another common way to organise the *cábalas* is through an index of revelations with each of their corresponding numbers.

4 "La 'bolita' en Cuba bate record después de la muerte de Fidel Castro", by Iván García, see www.radiotelevisionmarti.com/a/bolita-cuba-muerte-fidel-castro/134373.html. García's anecdote reveals how various types of events can influence interpretations of the *cábalas*.

5 Original version: "Lunes –Cifra que más discute el agua y el borracho 39-14-85 y cógelo que se te va."

6 Original version: "Martes –Cifra que más buscamos para hacer brujería y la paloma 49-53-80 y cógelo que se te va."

7 Penal Code of the Republic of Cuba, Chapter 13, Article 219.1.

8 For more information on the Lucky Strike Application, visit: "La 'bolita' cubana tiene su App" by Osniel Carmona Breijo, June 28, 2017, at this address: www.diariodecuba.com/cuba/1498676941_32204.html.

9 For more on the sonic attacks in Havana, see "The Mystery of the Havana Syndrome" (2018) by Adams Entous and Jon Lee Anderson published by *The New Yorker* and available here: www.newyorker.com/magazine/2018/11/19/the-mystery-of-the-havana-syndrome. A recent study argues that crickets might be the culprits of the sonic attacks, see "Crickets could be behind the Cuba "sonic attack' mystery, scientists say" by Tara John and published by CNN (January 7, 2019): www.cnn.com/2019/01/07/health/cuba-sonic-attack-crickets-scli-intl/index.html.

10 In his book *Sonic Warfare*, Steve Goodman (2009) shows that sonic technologies have been used for military purposes, including for torture and techniques of dissuasion.

## References

Barnet, Miguel. 1994. *Biography of a Runaway Slave*. Revised Edition. Willimantic: Curbstone Press.

Bronfman, Alejandra. 2016. *Isles of Noise: Sonic Media in the Caribbean*. Chapel Hill: The University of North Carolina Press.

Dunne, Anthony. 2005. *Hertzian Tales: Electronic Product, Aesthetic Experience, and Critical Design*. Cambridge: The MIT Press.

Frederick, Howard H. 1986. *Cuban American Radio Wars*. Norwood: Ablex Publishing Company.

Goodman, Steve. 2009. *Sonic Warfare: Sound, Affect, and the Ecology of Fear*. Cambridge: The MIT Press.

Holbraad, Martin. 2010. "The Whole Beyond Holism: Gambling, Divination, and Ethnography in Cuba." In *Experiments in Holism Theory and Practice in Contemporary Anthropology*, edited by Ton Otto and Nils Bubandt. Oxford: Wiley-Blackwell, pp. 67–85.

Saco, José Antonio. 1946. *La vagancia en Cuba*. Havana: Dirección de cultura.

Sáenz Rovner, Eduardo. 2008. *The Cuban Connection: Drug Trafficking, Smuggling, and Gambling in Cuba from the 1920s to the Revolution*. Chapel Hill: University of North Carolina Press.

# 5   Conga

Kelly was watching the Friday afternoon *telenovela* (soap opera) when she heard her neighbour yell from the other side of the street: "Kelly, telephone!" and she shouted back "I'm coming!" Kelly lives with her mother, Andrea, and her son Flavito. Like most of their neighbours, they do not have a landline telephone. They have to rely on their neighbour Orieta to receive and make calls. Orieta charges one Cuban peso every time people use her telephone. Those lucky enough to have a landline in Cuba often take advantage of this to make receiving phone calls for their neighbours into a small business. Orieta's phone is in her living room, placed on a coffee table beside a red imitation leather sofa. Today, her television set is turned on, and three adults siting in rocking chairs enjoy the last episode of *Caso Cerrado* (Case Closed, a programme broadcast by Telemundo during which the Cuban-American lawyer Ana María Polo arbitrates—and often ridicules—court cases). The neighbours are laughing at the current case and sharing unflattering comments about a lady who is accused of cheating on her husband in exchange for money. The living room is alive and noisy.

Kelly swiftly makes her way towards the phone (Illustration 5.1). Parking herself on the tip of Orieta's sofa, she grabs the telephone receptor and says in a jaded voice *dime* ("tell me"—what Cubans usually say when they respond to a telephone call). "Kelly, it's me Griselda [INAUDIBLE], we received the fabrics to finish the adornment of the dresses [INAUDIBLE], you can come today or tomorrow morning to pick them up. Your mother must be waiting [INAUDIBLE]." In response, Kelly nodded her head affirmatively, as the din around her did not allow for an audible verbal response. The lawyer of *Caso Cerrado* had given her final verdict about the unfaithful lady, and the neighbours sitting beside Kelly did not seem contented with her decision. Kelly hung up, left one Cuban peso on the coffee table, and greeted Orieta who was busy cooking in the kitchen.

*Illustration 5.1* Kelly using her neighbour's phone.

Kelly is one of my best friends, and we are *comadre* (meaning that I am the godmother of her child). Her mother Andrea is the president of a historical society called the *Tumba Francesa La Caridad de Oriente*. In 2005, UNESCO recognised this institution and its dances and songs as an "Intangible Heritage of Humanity." I have known Kelly and her family because of my undergraduate honours and Master's thesis research projects, which concerned the tumbas francesas in Eastern Cuba. I remember exactly the moment I first visited Kelly and her mother at the headquarters of the society. I was a young and inexperienced ethnographer, and I was intimidated by Andrea's grandeur, who had, and still has, a strong personality and is a central figure in the Tumba Francesa Society. But since then, our friendship has never stopped growing.

The tumbas francesas have a long and complex history in Cuba, and although they are not the main topic of the present story, a few things need to be mentioned. The tumba francesa societies emerged in the urban and semi-urban areas of Eastern Cuba after Emancipation around the end of the 19th century, as former slaves moved from rural plantations to towns and cities. These societies had their genesis on the coffee plantations of French landowners who had fled from the turmoil of the Haitian Revolution for Cuba almost a century earlier. The eastern part of Cuba was geographically close to the French colony of Saint-Domingue (which in 1804 became the independent nation of Haiti) and the price of land was more affordable than near Havana (Alén 1977). The language of communication on the French émigrés' coffee plantations in Cuba remained French or French Creole for more than a generation. So, slaves labouring on these plantations were thought of as "French" by their Cuban compatriots. These slaves, their descendants and slaves purchased in Cuba by the French owners created the tumba francesa societies. It is reported that in the 1950s, there were still more than 40 tumbas francesas in the regions of Santiago de Cuba and Guantánamo (Tamames 1961; Eli Rodríguez et al. 1997). Today, only three of them still exist: one called La Pompadour (later officially renamed Santa Catalina de Ricci) in the city of Guantánamo, the La Caridad de Oriente in Santiago de Cuba, and the third, a rural society, located in the mountain village of Bejuco in the municipality of Sagua de Tánamo in the province of Holguin.

Historically, the tumbas francesas emerged as societies of recreation, protection, and mutual aid, composed of slaves and free black people. Members paid monthly dues, which were accumulated to pay for members' funerals and burial costs or help peers in times of illness or financial need. In addition, these societies were important institutions sustaining the transmission of rituals, beliefs, and art forms across generations. Similar to other black mutual-aid societies in Cuba, the tumbas francesas had a hierarchical structure including an elected King (later called President) and Queen. After the Cuban Revolution in 1959, the new government decided to preserve the tumba francesa societies and promote them as part of the Cuban cultural kaleidoscope. However, the tumba francesa societies and other still-existing recreation and mutual aid societies lost some of their original function as providers of assistance during hardship. They were re-organised by the Cuban socialist government as folkloric or heritage preservation organisations. Now, the Ministry of Culture provides them with fabric for costumes, a rehearsal space, and arranges performance schedules at folklore festivals in different cities and provinces of Cuba.

The tumba francesa societies have played a key role in Santiago de Cuba's carnival for more than one hundred years. In Santiago de Cuba, the carnival takes place annually from July 19 to 26. During this highly popular event, the city is transformed to accommodate the festivities. Several major avenues are closed to vehicular traffic and temporarily converted to pedestrian arcades, where purveyors sell food and snacks from carts, beer dispensaries fill cups, and other venders sell trinkets and toys. Outdoor performance stages are erected and sound systems set up throughout the city. Near the old port on a boulevard that follows the bay, motorised floats (*carrozas*) feature gyrating dancers and singers. Marching groups of costumed dancers and percussionists, called *paseos* and *comparsas*, perform choreographies. Heritage societies also perform, including the Tumba Francesa Society, displaying their talents and parade in front of an official jury, the population, and visiting tourists. There is no significant reward for the winners except the symbolic recognition of being the best group of the year.

Months before the carnival, people are invited to register and join the members of the Tumba Francesa to form a bigger group called the "Tumba Francesa with its Tahona." Each competes against the others within their own category. The Tumba Francesa Society is in the centenary group category, along with two other societies, the Carabalí Isuama and the famous Conga Los Hoyos, which we will learn more about later in our story.

For the members of these parade groups, the carnival is a period of enjoyment and effervescence, but there is a lot of work to be done, sewing costumes and holding rehearsals. The Municipal Department of Culture supplies official carnival groups with costumes, accessories, and shoes. Traditional groups, like the Tumba Francesa Society, sew their costumes from the fabric provided with the help of designers and dressmakers hired by the Municipal Department of Culture. Yet most of the work, for example, preparation of the accessories (such as hats, flowers in fabric, fans, and banners) and the finishing of the dresses often fall on the shoulders of the heads of the parade groups, which in our story corresponds to Kelly and Andrea. This is why carnival does not rhyme with vacation for Kelly and Andrea, who are busy like bees, sewing over one hundred or so carnival costumes and their accessories for the members of the Tumba Francesa Society and its associated *comparsa* La Tahona.

When Kelly arrived back at her house after the phone call, she told Andrea about the additional fabric that had just arrived at the Municipal Department of Culture to finish the dresses and the accessories.

She also told her mother that she would go pick it up the next morning. However, Andrea, who had been waiting for the past two weeks to be able to finish the dress for the Queen, did not intend to delay. "Kelly, we can't wait until tomorrow!" she responded, and added, "the other *comparsas* will take the most beautiful pieces of fabric! You have to go now to pick the best!" Andrea needed something shiny and colourful to finish the final outfits. Kelly knew there was no point of resisting her mother. So she left right away for the Municipal Department of Culture, a 20 minutes walk from her home (Illustration 5.2). Just as Kelly was heading out the door, Andrea reminded her daughter to hurry up and not dally in the streets, as if she was still a child.

*Illustration 5.2*  As Kelly leaves for the Municipal Department of Culture, her mother Andrea warns her not to dawdle in the streets.

*Illustration 5.3* A motorcyclist almost hits Kelly as she steps out her door.

As soon as Kelly crossed the threshold, she was immersed in the hubbub of the city (Illustration 5.3). She barely had time to react as a motorcyclist whizzed past, driving so close to her front door that it almost hit her, leaving behind a smell of gasoline and the roaring of a two-stroke engine. Motorcycles are a common mode of transportation in Santiago, and function as local taxis, although they are dangerous. For ten Cuban pesos (about 50 cents USD), the biker drives his passenger to any destination within the city centre (prices increase for longer trips to outlying neighbourhoods). But Kelly did not have the money to pay for a *moto*, plus walking would refresh her after being inside her home.

Kelly lives in a working-class neighbourhood called Los Hoyos, considered one of the most iconic of Santiago, because locals proudly maintain many religious and cultural traditions (Millet, Brea and Ruiz Vila 1997). She was born in Los Hoyos, and her mother as well: they both embody its colourful idiosyncrasies. Kelly plays drums in the Tumba Francesa Society, she has been active since she was three years old. She never misses an opportunity to have fun with family and friends, especially when it involves touring with the Tumba Francesa Society to other cities and provinces.

As Kelly reached the next street, she crossed paths with a *pregonero* (see Chapter 4) selling *bizcochuelo*. These are a type of mango that is appreciated for their sweet yellow pulp and rich aroma, harvested in El Caney, a fertile region near Santiago (Illustration 5.4). *Pregoneros* walk the streets of the neighbourhoods, often with a horse and cart, singing about their wares to signal clients to come out of their houses and buy. They sing short refrains about what is offered for sale, such as "!Mango amarillo, mango de bizcochuelo, ya llego el mango!" (yellow mango, bizcochuelo mango, the mangos have arrived!) or "!oye, oye, mango bizcochuelo hay, el amarilo ya llego!" (listen, listen, there is mango bizcochuelo, the yellow one arrived!). At the same time as the *pregonero* tries to attract the attention of clients with vocal poetics,

*Illustration 5.4* Kelly hears the *pregonero*: "Yellow mango, bizcochuelo mango, the mangos have arrived!"

they also guide their horses: "!Caballo, caballo, fweeeet, caballo!" (Horse, horse, fweeeet [whistling], horse!). The *pregoneros* are part of the street symphony of Santiago. Other soundmakers contribute to the composition, such as the beeping of cars and motorcycles, or mobile bread vendors, who chant, "fweet! pan especial! mantequilla con pan especial!" (fweet! [whistle] special bread! special bread with butter!).

Once in a while, someone in a hurry calls to a *pregonero* from their doorstep, yelling "Mango! Mango!" The vendor halts, and there is an intermission in the background rhythm of Santiago's street symphony as the repetitive "clip clop" of horseshoes and the rattle of the cart on the pavement pauses. The client goes to meet the *pregonero*, bringing along their own container, selects the mangoes, chats with the vender, pays, and takes their wares back to the house. Then, "Caballo! Caballo! Fweeeet!" and the *pregonero* continues down the street.

The sound scholar Vincent Andrisani (2015) writes about *pregoneros* in Havana and the historical and sonic legacy left by the city's ice cream vendors. He argues that in order to experience a city like Havana, where sonic layers are intrinsically interwoven into the urban fabric, one has to pay attention to the open spaces of the built environment, including the dialogues, social interactions, and the sonic atmosphere (Andrisani 2015). Similar to Havana, the street vendors of Santiago de Cuba bring a vocal poesy to the urban space. Their art is often transmitted across generations.

Music is another form of sonic expression that is ubiquitous in Cuba (for Havana, see Dubinsky 2016). Santiago de Cuba is indisputably a musical city. It is perceived by many Cubans as the cradle of the island, producing the best musicians in Cuba's history. Santiago is the birthplace of *son* and *danzón*, two musical genres at the heart of Cuban national culture, and which are known as the ancestors of salsa and timba. Today, the city offers a number of live music venues, including the famous Casa de La Trova in the historic centre. Cubans also listen to recorded music. Loudly! There seem to be no half-hearted measures: when they press play, it becomes difficult to hear what anyone is saying, and very rarely will someone turn down the volume to make the conversation easier. Music played in taxis and buses is often played so loud that it is distorted. Music is part of the social landscape of close, intimate living: one cannot avoid it. Summers are hot in Santiago de Cuba, where the temperature easily reaches 40°C. Most families live in close quarters, and windows are open to catch every breeze (most do not have glass anyway). Music permeates the city from the sunrise to late at night. There are no official noise regulations implemented in Cuba as is common in North American and European cities. As in Edilberto's story (see Chapter 4), Cubans sit outside in the evening to escape the heat, sidewalks become living rooms, and the street becomes an orchestra of recorded music from the sound systems and of bicycle-taxis, to radio and television sets, to live music from venues as well as from religious meetings. Music is only one form of expression, many others contribute to the sonic architecture of the city.

As she walked by some domino players sitting in Serrano Park, a man in his sixties gazed at Kelly and told her, "¡Si cocinas como caminas, me comiera hasta la raspa!" (If you cook like you walk, I'd scrape the pot!). The man was still rubbernecking at her as he snapped his domino on the table making a loud *clap!* (Illustration 5.5). Kelly

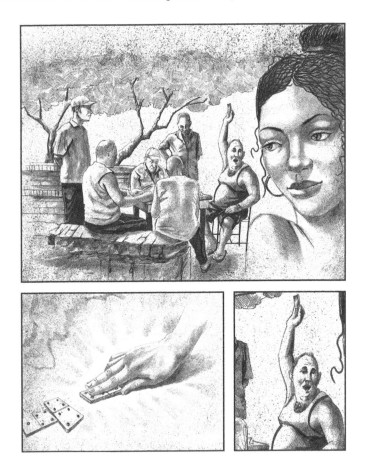

*Illustration 5.5* A man playing dominoes cat calls Kelly.

ignored him and continued her way. Not a day passes in her life without hearing *piropos* (cat calls) from men in the street. It is part of the daily experience of being in public spaces for Kelly and indeed all Cuban women. There are the various ubiquitous sounds made with the mouth: "tssssss," "psssssst," "fweeeeet," kisses, and muffled whispering tossed in to the air with the intention of praising a woman or attracting her attention. Some *piropos* are elaborate and relatively polite. Others are rude. Humorous, original, or particularly poetic *piropos* may occasionally snatch a smile from a recipient: "With so many curves, and me without breaks," or "You are so sweet that I gain weight just by looking at you," and "God, from which tree did this mango fall?" plus "You deserve being declared a National Treasure."[1] I also experienced hearing *piropos*, which I usually do not appreciate, but the most memorable one actually made me burst out laughing even if it was far from being flattering. As I passed by a man, he turned towards me and spontaneously said with a suave voice full of surprise and exclamation: "Ay mami (Hey mommy), your pants are exploding!" meaning that I had enough flesh to fill my pants in voluptuous shapes. Women walking in public in Cuba tend to adopt a blasé attitude towards *piropos*. Some hurry away, others smile, or exaggerate the sway of their hips, or even flirt back at the man by calling him *papi*, or *mi mangon* (my big mango). And many women do not restrain themselves from cat calling men![2] Kelly does not necessarily consider *piropos* offensive when she hears them. She says she would actually wonder if something was wrong with her appearance if a day went by with no man cat calling her.

Kelly was approaching the Municipal Department of Culture when drumming suddenly tickled her eardrums (Illustration 5.6). Travelling in the air above the roofs and between the buildings, the sonic waves made her whole body vibrate and the rhythm echoed her heart beats. What she heard could be nothing else than the conga! Congas are spontaneous parades happening in the streets. They are led by musicians in a conga organization, with participants joining the crowd along the way. The congas differ from the well-rehearsed and choreographed carnival *comparsas* discussed earlier. Congas are spontaneous events. Each conga is associated with a neighbourhood (Milstein 2013). There are currently six congas in Santiago de Cuba: San Pedrito, Alto Pino, El Tivolí, San Agustín, El Guayabito, and Los Hoyos. The congas, like the tumba francesa societies, emerged from the mutual aid societies of the 19th century in which slaves and free men met to share music and dances (Brea and Millet 1988; Zuñiga 2010; Castillo Masó 2013). Congas frequently "invade" the streets before and during

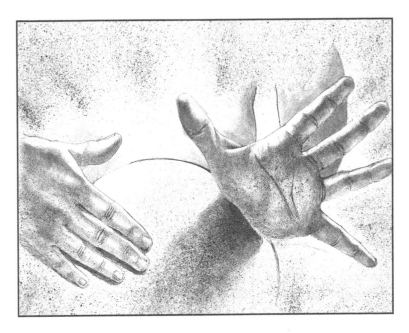

*Illustration 5.6*  Kelly can hear the conga nearby.

carnival with their percussion bands and hundreds of followers. The carnival of Santiago de Cuba is unofficially launched by an "invasion," which refers to a long parade led by the Conga Los Hoyos and followed by the other congas. The whole city is suddenly transformed into a gigantic street happening, a real "invasion." Also, congas may parade throughout the year to celebrate a happy event, most notably when the baseball team of Santiago de Cuba wins against the *Industriales*, the team from Havana.

Congas emerged within the unique demographics of Eastern Cuba, which were influenced by multiple waves of migration from Jamaica and Haiti (Milstein 2013). Although it is not rare to hear Cubans associate the conga with something that "Black people like to do" (*cosa de negro*), Lani Milstein (2013), who conducted extensive fieldwork on the congas in Santiago de Cuba, argues that the congas are most associated with the culture of the *santiaguero* (someone from Santiago, *cosa del santiaguero*). Therefore, she argues that congas might not necessarily break racial borders. Anthropologist Kristina Wirtz has a slightly different view on the topic. She writes that the *movement* of the congas parading through neighbourhoods considered more black or more white challenges the mappings of race and proposes a dynamic model of racialisation in action (Wirtz 2017:57). According to Wirtz, it is the *movement* of black bodies in different areas of the city that makes visible the racial dynamics taking place in the urban spaces of Santiago de Cuba.

The six existing congas in Santiago are located in neighbourhoods that tend to be more demographically black, more "traditional" (Millet, Brea and Ruiz Vila 1997), and more marginalised economically. Kristina Wirtz makes the point that by parading through neighbourhoods that are considered more white, the congas can destabilise the racial dynamics and demographics that are associated with each neighbourhood. However, racial segregation does not exist in Cuba to the same extent as most North American cities. Race in Cuba is complex, as is the issue of class, in part, because of the political landscape of the country and also because of historical conjunctures. I believe that it is inappropriate to look at race in Cuba through a North American lens.[3] As an abbreviated discussion, slavery in Cuba was abolished in 1886. Then, the country won its independence from Spain at the beginning of 1900, but true independence was thwarted by a powerful neighbour to the north, as the U.S. intervened in Cuba's domestic affairs and foreign policies. At the time, huge economic, social, and cultural discrepancies existed between black Cubans and white families, who owned most of the cultivable land. In the 1960s, Fidel Castro's revolutionary government took aim at eliminating economic classes (and by extension racism). It was believed that by establishing social and economic programmes, education, employment opportunities, and healthcare for all Cubans, racism would be eliminated. Thus, the revolutionary government imposed a silence on racial issues, to speak of it continuing was to impugn socialism.

The dissolution of the Soviet Union, the socialist island's main trading partner, led to a deep economic crisis in Cuba in the 1990s. During this time, the economic marginalisation by race worsened. For example, according to a 1990 U.S. census, 83.5% of Cuban immigrants in the U.S. identified as white (reported by de la Fuente 2001:319). Thus, black families in Cuba are statistically less likely to have relatives in Miami or Madrid who send remittances from abroad. In addition, non-whites are underrepresented in the tourist sector (de la Fuente 2001), which is the most lucrative form of legal employment on the island today. This unequal access to hard currencies accentuates a social divide along racial lines. As a consequence, many Afro-Cubans have turned towards the informal economy (from prostitution[4] to hustling to the black market) in order to acquire hard currency, accentuating the idea shared by many Cubans that blacks are criminals, lazy, and inefficient (Pérez Sarduy and Stubbs 2000; de la Fuente 2001; Hansing 2002). Unfortunately, the economic crisis of the 1990s and the social ills associated with it have taken on a racialised tone and character (Hansing 2002:69; Hernandez-Reguant 2009).

The congas are associated with black cultural practices, specifically from Santiago. It is not rare to hear *santiagueros* claim that they have the "conga in their blood." Congas are often characterised as unpredictable, violent, or dangerous—especially for women—not only amongst whites but also by blacks. But when observing a conga, one cannot miss the broad range of skin and hair colours that take part in the festive encounter. Congas are a cultural phenomenon that carry a long and complex history, and they certainly raise the question of Cuban racial dynamics.

The Conga Los Hoyos was celebrating the feast day of Saint John (June 24) by parading through Santiago's historic city centre. Kelly could not resist, it was stronger than her will. Despite her mother's admonishments, she stepped up her pace and began searching for the conga parade in the narrow streets of the city centre. She could hear its sounds echoing across buildings and rooftops. Where could it be? In which direction was it making its way? Following the sound of the drums, and other people, who like her were looking for the conga, she got closer and closer. The vibrations made her whole body move. Soon she was searching and dancing at the same time, her hips and arms swaying. As she turned a street corner, the sound of drums jumped out like a strong wind. She spied the tail of the conga, with

*Illustration 5.7* Kelly cannot resist, she joins a conga parading down the narrow streets of the historic city centre.

people following the musicians, dancing behind them in the street (Illustration 5.7). Others watched the conga from their balconies or rooftops, without joining in the parade, or, more fearful, closed their doors and windows.

A conga is led by a small group of musicians who move together, often in a circle. The *corneta china* ("Chinese trumpet") gives the conga a distinctive melodic-rhythmic pattern that calls the percussionists to join in (Pérez Fernández and Rodríguez González 2008). Other instruments include drums, *campanas* (cowbells), and idiophones made from the rims of car brakes, frying pans, or other metal items that can be hit to produce distinctive sounds. As the conga makes its way, the participants chant "catchy" phrases, such as "oye *Santiagueros* caminando, que bola?" (listen *Santiagueros* walking along, what's up?). The conga's chanting and instruments form a call-and-response. Participants who pour out of homes and buildings to follow the conga are said to be *arrollandose* (rolling along) as they sing and dance. The conga flows like a human tide made up of sweating, chanting, laughing, and yelling bodies. Occasionally, scuffles erupt, provoked by the heat and the crowding, mixed with too much rum and neighbourhood rivalries.

Kelly was getting close to finding the conga, she could see the crowd, and feel the heat emanating from bodies in the street. Kelly recognised the sound of the Conga Los Hoyos, a famous conga from her own neighbourhood! The Conga Los Hoyos and the Tumba Francesa Society are amongst the three remaining centenary societies still alive in Santiago de Cuba. Knowing that she would be rolling, or *arrollandose*, with her favourite conga added to her excitement (Illustration 5.8). She squeezed her way through the crowd up to the head of the conga, pushing close to the musicians, where the intensity was at the highest, so she could feel the sound vibrating through her body. After having danced and chanted until the conga dissipated, Kelly was exhausted and thirsty. Suddenly, she realised that it was too late to accomplish her task at the Municipal Department of Culture. Her mother was probably worried, waiting for her at home. She would have to go back to pick up the fabrics tomorrow.

The lyrics of the popular song "Añoranza por la conga" (Yearning for the conga) by Ricardo Leyva and his band Sur Caribe came to her mind. The song tells the story of a woman who left Santiago in search of another destiny. However, from far away, she keeps missing the conga and her homeland. Sur Caribe's lead singer, Ricardo Leyva, calls on *santiagueros* to enjoy their conga, their traditions: "I don't want any jams, any trouble, any loss of energy. After the conga, you'll

*Illustration 5.8* Kelly makes her way through the crowd up to the head of the conga and dances beside the musicians.

go back to work."[5] And this is what awaits Kelly. Her mother might not understand, but she does not regret her decision. The conga is in her blood: she is the conga.

## Conclusion

In Kelly's story, sound waves capture passers-by, convincing some of them to follow along with the conga as it "rolls" down the streets of Santiago. Kelly hears the call of the drums and follows. As she crosses different public spaces, Kelly meets various sources of sound, some enter in competition, whilst others complement each other in the creation of a spontaneous street symphony. Sounds invade a territory, and, as the conga, they are chopped by buildings, openings, and other sources of noise. They maintain boundaries between neighbourhoods and groups (also Oosterbaan 2009) and give shape to the urban experience of Santiago de Cuba. Travelling above the roofs and through the interstices of the city, the vibrations make their way to Kelly and also to the heart of the *santiagueros*. After the conga passes, the sounds of cars, *pregoneros*, music, and a few birds come back to create the everyday symphony of Santiago de Cuba.

## Notes

1 The original versions in Spanish: "Tú con tantas curvas y yo sin frenos," "Eres tan dulce, que sólo con mirarte engordo," "Dios, ¿y de qué mata se cayó ese mango?" and "Mereces ser declaradas Patrimonio Nacional."
2 Cat calling also takes place amongst the LGTB population, although I would argue that it is not that openly expressed.
3 See Baker (2011) who also discusses this issue.
4 There is a widespread consensus that most prostitutes (*jineteras*) are black or *mulatta* (De la Fuente 2001:326).
5 The original version in Spanish: "Que yo no quiero molote, ni quiero relajo, luego de la conga vallan pa'l trabajo." The Conga Los Hoyos collaborated with various music groups in Cuba, the most successful is the song they recorded with Ricardo Leyva mentioned here. The song won a Cubadisco award (similar to a Grammy) in 2006. They also recorded with the Canadian jazz musician Jane Bunnett. The new music director of the Conga, Lázaro Banderas, son of general director Félix Banderas, is in large part responsible for new music connections with Cuban popular music which have rejuvenated the Conga Los Hoyos and increased its visibility in the country and abroad.

## References

Alén Rodriguez, Olavo. 1977. "Las sociedades de tumba francesa en Cuba." *Santiago* 25:193–209.
Andrisani, Vincent. 2015. "The Sweet Sounds of Havana: Space, Listening, and the Making of Sonic Citizenship." *Sounding Out!* September 17, 2015. Available at: https://soundstudiesblog.com/2015/09/17/the-sweet-sounds-of-havana-space-listening-and-the-making-of-sonic-citizenship/
Baker, Geoff. 2011. *Buena Vista in the Club: Rap, Reggaetón, and Revolution in Havana.* Durham: Duke University Press.
Brea, Rafael and José Millet. 1988. "Presencia africana en los carnavales de Santiago de Cuba." *África: Revista do Centro de Estudos Africanos* 11(1):121–136.
Castillo Masó, Anisley Caridad. 2013. "Arrolando con la Conga de San Pedrito en Santiago de Cuba." *Batey: Revista Cubana de Antropología Sociocultural* V(5):18–32. Available at: www.revista-batey.com/index.php/batey/article/view/46.

de la Fuente, Alejandro. 2001. *A Nation for All: Race, Inequality, and Politics in Twentieth Century Cuba*. Chapel Hill: The University of North Carolina Press.

Dubinsky, Karen. 2016. *Cuba Beyond the Beach: Stories of Life in Havana*. Toronto: Between the Lines.

Eli Rodríguez, Victoria et al. 1997. *Instrumentos de la música folclórico-popular de Cuba*. Volume 1. La Habana: Editorial de Ciencias Sociales.

Hansing, Katrin. 2002. *Rasta, Race and Revolution: The Emergence and Development of the Rastafari Movement in Socialist Cuba*. DPhil thesis. University of Oxford.

Hernandez-Reguant, Adriana. 2009. "Writing the Special Period: An Introduction." In *Cuba in the Special Period: Culture and Ideology in the 1990s*, edited by Ariana Hernandez-Reguant. New York: Palgrave Macmillan, pp. 1–18.

Milstein, Lani. 2013. "Toward an Understanding of Conga Santiaguera: Elements of La Conga Los Hoyos." *Latin American Music Review* 34(2): 223–254.

Millet, José, Rafael Brea and Manuel Ruiz Vila. 1997. *Barrio, comparsa y carnaval Santiaguero*. Santiago de Cuba: Ediciones Casa del Caribe.

Oosterbaan, Martijn. 2009. "Sonic Supremacy: Sound, Space and Charisma in a Favela in Rio de Janeiro." *Critique of Anthropology* 29(1):81–104.

Pérez Fernández, Rolando and Santiago Rodríguez González. 2008. "La corneta china (suona) en Cuba: Una contribución cultural asiática trascendente." *Afro-Hispanic Review* 27(1):139–160.

Pérez Sarduy, Pedro and Jean Stubbs. 2000. *Afro-Cuban Voices: On Race and Identity in Contemporary Cuba*. Miami: University Press of Miami.

Tamames, Elisa. 1961. "Antecedentes sociologicos des las tumbas francesas." *Actas del Folklore* 1(10–12):25–32.

Wirtz, Kristina. 2017. "Mobilizations of Race, Place, and History in Santiago de Cuba's Carnivalesque." *American Anthropologist* 119(1):58–72.

Zuñiga, Olga Portuondo. 2010. "El Carnaval Santiaguero, origen y Resistencia." *Revista Brasileira do Caribe* X(20):475–484.

# Conclusion

Alexis is a beekeeper. His house is located between the Sierra Maestra mountains and the ocean (Illustration C.1). The scenic ride from the provincial capital of Santiago de Cuba to the hamlet where Alexis lives takes approximately 45 minutes. In addition to taking care of his bees, Alexis is also a veterinarian and a carpenter. I began to be interested in beekeeping as part of my aerial imagination research project and decided to conclude this book with something Alexis told me during

*Illustration C.1*  Alexis's hives in the Sierra Maestra mountains.

one of our conversations, and which was one of those "high-revealing-moments" of my fieldwork.

In Cuba, the beekeeping industry is nationalised. Honey is collected after the harvesting season by officers from the Ministry of Agriculture. The Ministry takes care of the pasteurisation and commercialisation of honey as well as the production of various derivatives used for natural medicine. Equipment and technical support are provided to the beekeepers who follow the hygienic and reproductive standards established by the Ministry.

There are three main types of bees in a hive: the queen and the workers (all females) and the drones (all males). The queen has a very special role. She is one of a kind, the mother of all the bees in the hive, the centre of the colony, and the seed of modern apiculture (Verde Jiménez et al. 2013). The queen is responsible for laying the eggs to insure the continuous reproduction of the bees, whilst the workers take care of feeding her and getting rid of her waste.

A queen bee lives an average of one to five years. In Cuba, beekeepers can buy queen bees from the municipal office of the Ministry of Agriculture thanks to the Cuban Genetic Improvement Programme. The Ministry recommends replacing the queen bee every year to secure the quality and variety of genetics, as well as the production of the hives (Verde Jiménez et al. 2013). The switch to a new queen can also happen without the input of the beekeeper (or the Cuban Ministry of Agriculture). Similar to a *coup d'état*, the queen can be replaced when the workers decide that she is too old, disabled, and/or failing: if her productivity diminishes. Swarming is another process through which a queen bee is replaced by a younger virgin queen. It occurs when the hive is too crowded or when weather conditions are appropriate, usually in springtime. When a swarm is immanent, the queen lays eggs in a few "queen cups," created by workers to raise future queens. They are fed with royal jelly, a different diet than what is provided to the other bees. Their special diet explains why the queens are bigger than the rest of the population in the hive. The first queen to escape her cell kills all of her young sisters. Only one queen will survive.

Just before the new virgin queen emerges from her cell and fights for her life, the old queen leaves the hive with the prime swarm (Illustration C.2). A large group of worker bees from the hive follows her to help restart a new colony in another location. A few days after birth, ideally on a dry, warm, and sunny day, the young virgin queen momentarily leaves the hive for fecundation. She mates with 12 to 15 drones, whose fate is to die afterwards (after, she kills them with her sting). Mating takes place whilst flying in high altitudes, in what is

*Illustration C.2* The first flight of the new virgin queen.

known in the apiculture world as a "drone congregation area." After the mating, the queen returns to the hive and begins to lay eggs.

Alexis knows all of this, and much more. He has spent many hours explaining the intricacies of beekeeping to me, an occupation he cherishes. I visited his hives a few times with the use of a smoker and some basic protection equipment. I remain deeply impressed by the complexity of beekeeping, but more so, of the ease with which Alexis manipulates the bees without protection and with his bare hands. He quietly talks to the bees. His body moves around softly, as if he is also airborne. He is convinced that his bees recognise him—which explains why they do not often sting him.

One day, while sitting in his carpentry shop, Alexis told me about the virgin bee and the process through which a new queen becomes the head of a hive through the swarming process. This was a lot to take in for someone who knew little about beekeeping and I was not recording our conversation. However, I wish to report a few sentences Alexis told me that day, which still resonate in my head when I think about aerial imagination.

He said: "...the virgin queen flies towards the sky until she reaches a very high altitude, some say as high as three to four kilometers up. The drones follow behind her. She hovers there in the *espacio vital* (vital space)."

When I heard this concept, made of two simple words, *espacio vital*, I stopped breathing. After Alexis repeated the expression—at my request—I could not help but think that this term conveyed exactly the Cuban aerial imagination. It refers to a life-and-death space, something that is absolutely necessary. It also represents an aerial source of complete energy that is lively and swarming with activity and movement. At this moment, all the dots connected in my head, as if a celestial map had been laid down in front of my eyes. This is when I fully grasped the meaning of "aerial imagination," not only my interpretation of what I gathered from my ethnographic explorations and my seemingly eclectic themes of research, but, even more powerfully, how *I* came to imagine the Cuban aerial space as fully enmeshed in all dimensions. The sky opened up in front of me as I connected the various aerial practices, activities, and beliefs associated with human and non-human agents, as well as their relationships with various material objects that constitute everyday life. The aerial space is all about circulation and movement: mobility allows the reproduction of life. My brain was bubbling.

It was also at that precise moment that I came back to the beginning, to the story of Our Lady of Charity of El Cobre that is so dear to the heart of Cubans (discussed in the Introduction). With my imagination still going wild, I juxtaposed the queen bee story to the iconography associated to the legend of Our Lady of Charity. The queen bee and the Virgin of Charity merged to become the mother of all Cubans (Illustration C.3). Their strength stood firmly and in the power of the *espacio vital*, in the sky above, as they fulfilled their role of protectors and reproducers of life. Many other interpretations and metaphors could emerge from this rich visual representation. But what I wish to emphasise here is how concepts shared with me during informal conversations with Cuban friends and participants in my research project pushed my reflections of the Cuban sky to another level. In a poetic and even playful manner, my brain grasped the freedom to interpret what I heard and observed whilst conducting fieldwork. I came to full realisation that the Cuban aerial space is a vital space and that this characteristic was the glue that made all the elements I gathered during my research stick together (paraphrasing Barber 2007). The concept of vital space was essential to my project.

*Illustration C.3* The new queen hovering in vital space.

It is with my feet back on the ground that I reflect again on what wi-fi antennas, cactuses, pigeons, the lottery, congas, and bees have in common. It is my hope that in placing these unexpected combinations of concerns beside each other, I provided a sense of how the sky allows forms of circulation to happen. The sky is a space of circulation, and a multitude of information travels through the air. Thus, it can be understood as a *medium*, defined as a vehicle that carries meaning (Durham Peters 2015).

If we dig a little bit deeper into the idea that the sky is a medium or a milieu (in an ecological sense), and in following the argument developed by the philosopher John Durham Peters (2015), we can enlarge our horizons of what constitutes media. This includes not only antennas, cell phones, and radio sets, but, more inclusively, natural and cultural systems that allow goods, objects, and, by extension, systems of beliefs to circulate. The sky becomes a social space of circulation and interaction that allows things, people, and animals to connect and exchange. I like to think of the sky as offering an "infrastructure of circulation," like cables that allow electricity to travel or drains let water flow. Indeed, for many people, infrastructure remains a technical and even military term, yet this book does not focus on the technocratic aspects of infrastructure. Rather, this collection of stories looks at how infrastructures mediate the social (Larkin 2008) and how they are linked to fantasy, imagination, and ideology (Humphrey 2005), aesthetics, and poetics (Larkin 2013). The five stories developed in this book were not limited to the "built infrastructures" made by humans (antennas, cables, etc.), but included other types of systems that make things happen in the sky, for instance, religion and animal forms of orientation. This inclusive view contributes to a non-human–centric perspective on media infrastructure and circulation.

In approaching the sky as a medium in which information circulates in all directions, this book reclaims a space of critical engagement formerly left to dreamers or aeronautical engineers. My stories attempt to demonstrate that the aerial imagination is intertwined with the politics of place, economy, and race. The sky is a historically and culturally constructed concept that is interpreted and imagined in various ways. It is changeable, and it speaks to a historical moment (Durham Peters 2015:49). Instead of looking in one typical direction down towards the ground, as it is most often the case when thinking about aerial imagination or "aerial view" (see, for instance, de Certeau 1984), this book encourages readers to turn their gaze towards the sky, a celestial territory that is all around us, even inside our lungs, but also above our reach.

When we think about circulation and flow, we also need to acknowledge friction and the various speeds at which things circulate (or not) in the sky. Chapter 1, for instance, touches on the alternative systems developed by Cubans to share digital information through ethernet cables and illicit wi-fi connections. These networks emerged because of the unreliability of official systems of communication. It is digital scarcity that has pushed Cubans to invent new aerial media to share information through the sky. New forms of circulation are spurred by frictions (Tsing 2005; see also Born 2005) but also act as a creative force (Boudreault-Fournier 2016). As suggested by the story developed in Chapter 1, scarcity and inaccessibility can inspire creative agency that encourages the adoption of means, techniques, and approaches to fix (*resolver*) problems.

Wi-fi antennas, cactuses, pigeons, the lottery, congas, and bees are all connected to vital space and the aerial imagination—at different speeds and in spite of various forms of tensions and resistance. The Cuban sky is a culturally embedded space of swarming activity and movement that is different from other aerial spaces elsewhere in the world. My ethnographic gaze, rotated towards the sky, allowed the emergence of this assemblage, made of objects, humans, animals, dreams, and thoughts. Hopefully, *Aerial Imagination in Cuba* encourages readers to direct their gaze towards imagined spaces or media and to potentially rethink the ways in which we typically assemble our material and immaterial worlds.

## References

Barber, Karin. 2007. "Improvisation and the Art of Making Things Stick." In *Creativity and Cultural Improvisation*, edited by Elizabeth Hallam and Tim Ingold. Oxford: Berg, pp. 25–41.

Born, Georgina. 2005. "On Musical Mediation: Ontology, Technology and Creativity." *Twentieth-Century Music* 2(1):7–36.

Boudreault-Fournier, Alexandrine. 2016. "The Fortune of Scarcity: Digital Music in Circulation." In *The Routledge Companion to Digital Ethnography*, edited by Larissa Hjorth et al. New York: Routledge, pp. 344–353.

de Certeau, Michel. 1984. *The Practice of Everyday Life*. Berkeley: University of California Press.

Durham Peters, John. 2015. *The Marvelous Clouds: Toward A Philosophy of Elemental Media*. Chicago: The University of Chicago Press.

Humphrey, Caroline. 2005. "Ideology in Infrastructure: Architecture and Soviet Imagination." *Royal Anthropological Institute* 11:39–58.

Larkin, Brian. 2008. *Signal and Noise: Media, Infrastructure, and Urban Culture in Nigeria*. Durham: Duke University Press.

Larkin, Brian. 2013. "The Politics and Poetics of Infrastructure." *Annual Review of Anthropology* 42:327–343.

Tsing, Anna Lowenhaupt. 2005. *Friction: An Ethnography of Global Connection*. Princeton: Princeton University Press.

Verde Jiménez, Mayda, Jorge Demedio Lorenzo and Tomás Gómez Bernia. 2013. *Apicultura: Salud y produción. Guía técnica para el apicultor*. La Habana: Instituto de Medicina Veterinaria, Ministerio de la Agricultura.

# Index

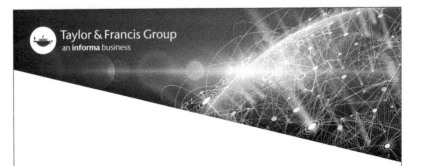

For Product Safety Concerns and Information please contact our EU
representative GPSR@taylorandfrancis.com
Taylor & Francis Verlag GmbH, Kaufingerstraße 24, 80331 München, Germany

www.ingramcontent.com/pod-product-compliance
Ingram Content Group UK Ltd.
Pitfield, Milton Keynes, MK11 3LW, UK
UKHW021422080625
459435UK00011B/116

* 9 7 8 0 3 6 7 7 8 7 8 9 9 *